National Parks Centennial

1885

1985

Centenaire des parcs nationaux

100 years of heritage conservation

A special production of
PARKS CANADA
ATLANTIC REGION
in honour of The National Parks Centennial

ATLANTIC CANADA'S
Natural Heritage Areas

BY
ROGER M. BEARDMORE

©**Minister of Supply and Services Canada 1985**

Available in Canada through
Authorized Bookstore Agents
and other bookstores
or by mail from
Canadian Government Publishing Centre
Supply and Services Canada
Ottawa, Canada K1A 0S9

Catalogue No. R62-222/1985 E
ISBN 0-660-11787-8

Canada: $14.95   Other Countries: $17.95
Price subject to change without notice

ATLANTIC CANADA'S
Natural Heritage Areas

Foreword 7	Federal Migratory Bird Sanctuaries 38
Acknowledgements 9	Grand Manan 38
National Parks 10	Machias Seal Island 39
	Amherst Point 39
Kouchibouguac 10	Haley Lake 40
Fundy 13	Port Joli and Port Hebert 40
Kejimkujik 15	Big Glace Bay Lake 41
Cape Breton Highlands 16	Kentville 41
Prince Edward Island 18	Sable River 41
Gros Morne 20	Sable Island 42
Terra Nova 22	Black Pond 43
	Terra Nova 43
Natural Areas of Canadian Significance 25	Provincial Parks 46
Deer Island 25	New Brunswick 46
Grand Manan 26	Nova Scotia 52
Brier Island 26	Prince Edward Island 59
Cape La Have Islands 26	Newfoundland and Labrador 62
Baie d'Espoir 27	
Mealy Mountains 27	Ecological Reserves 67
Torngat Mountains 28	New Brunswick 68
	Nova Scotia 72
Canadian Heritage Rivers 30	Prince Edward Island 76
St. Croix River 30	Newfoundland and Labrador 78
National Wildlife Areas 32	Provincial Wildlife Management Areas/ Wildlife Refuges/Game Sanctuaries 84
Portage Island 32	
Portobello Creek 33	New Brunswick 84
Shepody 33	Nova Scotia 86
Tintamarre 34	Prince Edward Island 88
Cape Jourimain 34	
Chignecto 35	Summary and Conclusions 90
Wallace Bay 35	Selected References 92
Margaree Island 35	
Boot Island 36	
Sand Pond 36	
Port Joli and Port Hebert 36	

LIST OF TABLES

TABLE 1	National Parks	24
TABLE 2	Natural Areas of Canadian Significance	29
TABLE 3	Canadian Heritage Rivers	30
TABLE 4	National Wildlife Areas	37
TABLE 5	Federal Migratory Bird Sanctuaries	45
TABLE 6	Rest Area Parks — New Brunswick	47
TABLE 7	Campground Parks — New Brunswick	48
TABLE 8	Beach Parks — New Brunswick	49
TABLE 9	Recreation Parks — New Brunswick	50
TABLE 10	Wildlife Parks — New Brunswick	51
TABLE 11	Resource Parks — New Brunswick	51
TABLE 12	Campground Parks — Nova Scotia	53
TABLE 13	Picnic and Beach Parks — Nova Scotia	54
TABLE 14	Wildlife Parks/Historic Parks/Boat Ramps — Nova Scotia	58
TABLE 15	Provincial Parks — Prince Edward Island	60
TABLE 16	Camping Parks — Newfoundland and Labrador	63
TABLE 17	Day Use Parks — Newfoundland and Labrador	65
TABLE 18	Natural Scenic Attractions — Newfoundland and Labrador	66
TABLE 19	Ecological Reserves — New Brunswick	69
TABLE 20	Candidate Ecological Reserves — New Brunswick	70
TABLE 21	Candidate Ecological Reserves — Nova Scotia	73
TABLE 22	Candidate Natural Areas — Prince Edward Island	76
TABLE 23	Ecological Reserves — Newfoundland and Labrador	79
TABLE 24	Candidate Ecological Reserves — Newfoundland and Labrador	80
TABLE 25	Wildlife Refuges — New Brunswick	85
TABLE 26	Wildlife Management Areas — New Brunswick	85
TABLE 27	Game Sanctuaries — Nova Scotia	87
TABLE 28	Wildlife Management Areas — Nova Scotia	87
TABLE 29	Wildlife Management Areas — Prince Edward Island	89
TABLE 30	Natural Heritage Areas — Occurrence by Province	90
TABLE 31	Natural Heritage Areas — Total Size by Province	91

Foreword

1985 marks the one hundredth anniversary of the creation of the first national park in Canada. Banff National Park in Alberta was set aside in 1885 in order to ensure continuing access by the people of Canada to an important part of their natural heritage. Parks Canada continues to work towards the completion of a national park system which will truly represent the country's richness and diversity. Today there are thirty-one national parks representing every province and territory and in area, Canada's national park system is one of the world's largest. The provinces and territories have also contributed significantly to the protection of natural areas for the benefit and enjoyment of Canadians.

Nature's bounty within Atlantic Canada is manifested by the presence of over six hundred natural heritage areas. Most of these are protected within the system of national and provincial parks, national wildlife areas, federal migratory bird sanctuaries, provincial game sanctuaries and ecological reserves. The establishment of these preserves indicates the commitment of both the federal and provincial governments to maintain and protect our natural heritage.

We have come a long way in the past one hundred years, but there is still much to be accomplished. All natural heritage areas together represent less than two percent of the land surface of Atlantic Canada. The national parks centennial marks an appropriate occasion to review what has been achieved, and to consider what remains to be done. This report's text, tables and maps illustrate the type and extent of natural areas which have been identified in the Atlantic Region as outstanding and special examples of our natural heritage. You are urged to visit and enjoy these areas in ways which will leave them unimpaired for generations to come.

Dr. C. J. Edmonds,
Regional Director-General,
Atlantic Region,
Environment Canada

Mr. W. C. Turnbull,
Regional Director,
Atlantic Region,
Parks Canada

Acknowledgements

The production of this report required a great deal of assistance. I would like to thank those whose help and guidance contributed so much to its completion.

Parks Canada
Neil Munro, Assistant Director, Operations, provided overall guidance and support for the project and his timely suggestions were vital to its production. Thanks go to Ian Church who originated the idea of a heritage places map and report. Both he and Paul Olshefsky assisted greatly in getting the project underway. Doug Kolmer, Chief, Interpretation, helped to guide the project through its final stages until printing and Roger Gaudet provided creative input to the layout of the report.

Energy, Mines and Resources Canada
Roger Marleau and Jack Weedmark of EMR's contract administration staff provided guidance in the planning of the natural heritage areas map, and administered its actual production.

New Brunswick
Mel Fitton and Jeff Patch, Fish and Wildlife Branch, Department of Natural Resources, provided information on the ecological reserves and wildlife reserves respectively, of the province of New Brunswick. Jean Paul Robichaud of the Crown Lands branch also provided assistance. Janet McNeil of the New Brunswick Legislative Library spent many hours researching the dates of establishment of the provincial game refuges and game management areas. Phil Ossinger and Kirby Burtt of the Parks Division, Department of Tourism, provided complete documentation on the provincial parks of New Brunswick. Penny Demmings, Promotion Officer, Tourism New Brunswick, supplied a selection of high quality photographs.

Nova Scotia
Brian Kinsman, Parks Division, Department of Lands and Forests, supplied all documentation and location maps for the provincial parks in Nova Scotia. Derek Davis and Robert Ogilvie of the Nova Scotia Museum provided information and photographs of the candidate ecological reserves in Nova Scotia.

Fred Payne and George Boyd of the Wildlife Division, Department of Lands and Forests, and Rob Doiron of Maritime Resource Management Service, contributed information on the game sanctuaries and wildlife management areas of Nova Scotia.

Prince Edward Island
Bruce Smith, Supervisor, Parks Programming, Department of Transportation and Public Works, supplied documentation on the provincial parks and candidate natural areas of Prince Edward Island as well as the background to their development. Randy Dibblee, Fish and Wildlife Division, Department of Community and Cultural Affairs, supplied information on provincial wildlife management areas.

Newfoundland and Labrador
Ken Curnew, Wildlands biologist, Department of Culture, Recreation and Youth, provided up-to-date information on the Wilderness and Ecological Reserves program in Newfoundland. Dr. Don Steele, Biology Department, Memorial University, supplied missing information on the IBP sites in Labrador. Glen Ryan, Chief of Planning and Development, Parks Division, supplied current and historical details of the Newfoundland and Labrador provincial parks system.

Others
Al Smith of the Canadian Wildlife Service provided complete information on national wildlife areas and federal migratory bird sanctuaries. Judy Dunn of Manpower Temporary Services and Wayne Lovett of Temporarily Yours employment agency contributed several days work compiling lists of information and meticulously plotting areas on the natural heritage areas map. Betty Hamilton and Nellie Balch assisted by preparing, typing and cross-checking lists of areas. Margaret McKee provided early editorial advice and comments. Jenny Winder, word processor operator, spent many hours inputting and re-processing several subsequent drafts. Debora Pollock Post provided professional editing and proofreading services.

Finally, I would like to thank Mr. W. C. Turnbull, Regional Director, Parks Canada and Dr. Clinton J. Edmonds, Regional Director-General, Atlantic Region, Environment Canada, for their sustained support of my assignment as Environment Canada's Centennial Coordinator.

Roger M. Beardmore
Environment Canada Centennial Coordinator
March, 1985

National Parks

National parks are special places intended to protect representative examples of the diversity of Canada's landscape and marinescape for the benefit of current and future generations. To this end, Parks Canada has divided Canada into sixty-eight natural regions, of which thirty-nine are terrestrial and twenty-nine are marine. Each of these natural regions should be represented in the system of national parks. Currently, there are thirty-one national parks in Canada covering an area of approximately 140,000 square kilometres. While significant, this represents fewer than half of the natural regions of Canada. Efforts are continuing therefore to identify new candidate areas and to establish national parks in under-represented regions.

National Parks are established by formal ammendment to the National Parks Act (1930), requiring open debate in the House of Commons. The Act completely prohibits resource developments. Section 4 states: "The Parks are hereby dedicated to the people of Canada for their benefit, education and enjoyment, subject to the provisions of this Act and the Regulations, and such Parks shall be maintained and made use of so as to leave them unimpaired for the enjoyment of future generations".

National parks protect part of the heritage of all Canadians. They offer a range of opportunities to learn about and enjoy the natural environment. In order to enable the continued protection of these areas, zones are identified within each park which reflect the degree of resource protection required and the type and intensity of visitor use that is appropriate. In this way a balance can be achieved between visitor use and wilderness preservation within each national park.

In the Atlantic Region there are seven national parks. Cape Breton Highlands (1936) was the first one, followed closely by Prince Edward Island (1937). The other parks were established as suitably representative land became available.

Kouchibouguac National Park, New Brunswick

Kouchibouguac National Park was established in 1969 to preserve a representative sample of the Maritimes Plain natural region. It covers 238 square kilometres consisting of an intricate blend of coastal and inland habitats, beaches, sand dunes, lagoons, salt marshes, bogs, rivers, forests and fields.

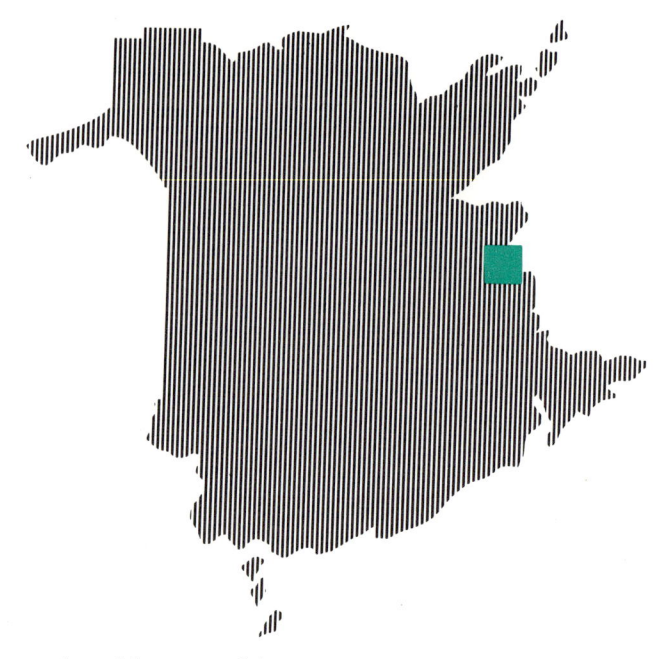

Age-old camps of the Micmac Indians preceded the settlements of early Acadians. The United Empire Loyalists followed while today the areas' character is once more predominantly Acadian.

The park's twenty-five kilometres of beach-fronted barrier islands have survived the centuries despite constant shifting from the push of wind and water. The forests of the interior are the backdrop to salt marshes which border the lagoons. These forests contain numerous wetland bogs and cedar swamps.

Flowing gently through the park are the St. Louis, the Black and the Kouchibouguac Rivers. The latter gives the park its name, and is derived from the Micmac word "Pee-chee-bou-guac" meaning "River of the long tides".

Different habitats support different forms of life. Along the coast, Tern Island is home to one of the largest common tern nesting sites in North America. A herd of grey and harbour seals can often be found at the mouth of the St. Louis River. The lagoons and salt marshes, productive nurseries for marine life, give food and shelter to resident seabirds and tens of thousands of migratory shorebirds, geese and ducks. Species such as the piping plover and the osprey (the park symbol) nest here. Inland, the forest supports many of the mammals common to eastern Canada including moose, deer, black bear, beaver, fox, hare, groundhog, porcupine and most recently, coyote. The bogs and cedar swamps harbour unusual and exotic life forms such as carnivorous pitcher plants and twenty-five species of wild orchid.

Saltmarsh and lagoon, Kouchibouguac National Park

Point Wolfe River at high tide, Fundy National Park

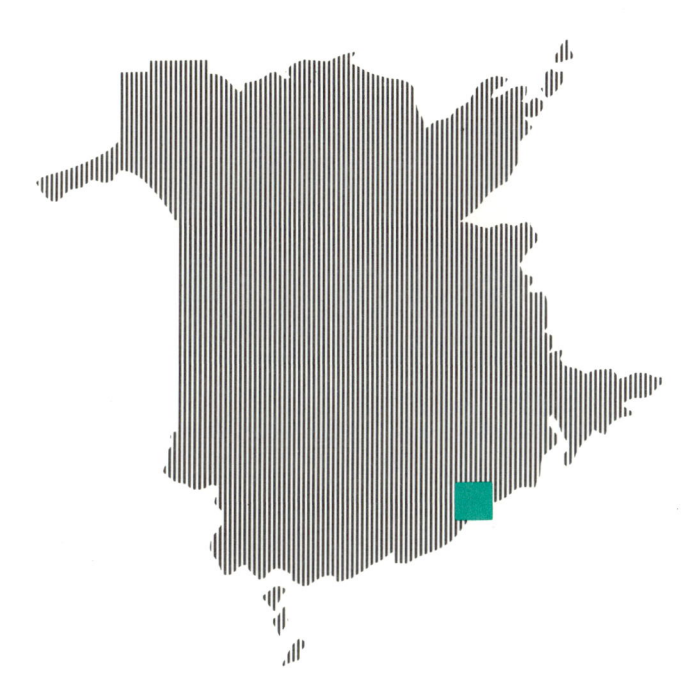

Fundy National Park, New Brunswick

Established in 1948, Fundy National Park covers 206 square kilometres along the Bay of Fundy shore in southern New Brunswick. It extends inland for more than 14.5 kilometres and skirts the Bay of Fundy for thirteen kilometres.

The Bay of Fundy is associated with some of Canada's earliest history. French and Portuguese fishermen visited the area in the 16th Century and it is believed that the modern name Fundy is derived from the Portuguese "Rio Fondo", meaning deep river. In 1604, Samuel de Champlain visited the Bay, claiming it as part of the French colony of Acadia which was later to become Nova Scotia under British rule. In 1784, what is now the Province of New Brunswick separated from Nova Scotia.

Rising and falling twice daily, the Bay of Fundy's tides are among the highest in the world. The average tidal difference along the shore of Fundy National Park ranges from six to twelve metres. The park faces the sea along a line of steep cliffs ranging from eighteen to sixty metres high, cut at intervals by streams entering the bay in deep valleys. Behind the wave-pounded cliffs the land rises in a rolling plateau, a remnant of an ancient range of mountains called the Caledonia Highlands. Averaging three hundred metres above sea level, the plateau is cut by deep valleys with steep, rocky walls and waterfalls. A few small lakes and swampy areas are found in the northwest section of the park.

Exposed in roadcuts and valley walls, the bed-rock is composed mainly of lava and ancient sediments which have been greatly altered during five hundred million years of existence. With the retreat of the last Ice Age about ten thousand years ago, the area was covered with a blanket of rock debris called glacial till from which most of the stony soils have developed.

The park's valleys and rounded hills contain varied vegetation, dominated by a mixture of broadleaved and evergreen trees. Along the coast where summers are cool, yellow and white birch are scattered among red spruce and balsam fir. The warmer plateau is dominated by stands of sugar maple, beech and yellow birch. Red spruce, balsam fir and red maple thrive in low, swampy areas.

The snowshoe hare, porcupine, beaver, red squirrel, chipmunk and woodchuck are some of the most frequently seen animals. The shy and secretive bobcat is rarely spotted. An eastern race of the coyote has recently been reported in the area, biologically replacing the native wolf which has been extinct for over a century. The last of the woodland caribou in the park were seen here about 1950. Though a few black bear travel through the park area, it is unlikely that any are resident. There are periodic sightings of the elusive eastern panther, giving hope that this extremely rare, endangered species may yet survive in or near Fundy National Park.

Over two hundred species of birds are recorded in Fundy and about ninety are known to nest in the park. The Bay of Fundy's shoreline is a migration route so that in the spring and fall large numbers of migrating species stop over in the park.

Speckled trout populate practically all the park's streams and lakes and toward the end of August, Atlantic salmon begin their spawning run up the Alma, one of it's rivers.

Mouth of Grafton Brook, Kejimkujik National Park

Kejimkujik National Park, Nova Scotia

Kejimkujik is a gently-rolling landscape in the southwest interior of Nova Scotia, with numerous lakes interconnected by smooth-flowing rivers. The park sustains in its 381 square kilometres, a diversity of wildlife inhabiting a variety of woodlands and dark waters.

The park was named after its largest lake, Kejimkujik (a Micmac Indian word pronounced "Kej-im-koo-jik", meaning "swollen area"). Native tribes have travelled through and inhabited Kejimkujik for over three thousand years. These woods were the seasonal home of the nomadic Micmac Indians for hundreds of years before the first Europeans came to Canada.

By the early 1820's, nearby communities were settled and a few farms were cleared in the area now included in the park. These early settlers mixed farming with lumbering, hunting and trapping to carve out a living.

The Kejimkujik wilderness became widely known as a sportsman's paradise. Resorts and cottages offered accommodation and supplied guides to visiting sportsmen and their families. By 1968, when Kejimkujik National Park was created, both the farming and wilderness resort eras were in decline.

Kejimkujik is underlain by ancient rocks which have been flattened and smoothed by glaciers. Dozens of low oval hills were formed and shallow basins were scoured in the bedrock. With the melting of the glaciers, water filled the shallow basins, forming the lake-studded landscape of today.

Kejimkujik's lush woodlands may be deceiving. Almost the entire park area has been burned or logged within the past two hundred years. Owing to the favourable climate however, regeneration has been rapid and forest now covers ninety percent of the land.

Mixed woods comprise about three-quarters of the park forests while conifers cover about one-fifth of the park. Red maple, red oak and white birch occur on dry locations, while pure stands of white and red pine often grow near lakeshores. Eastern hemlock groves, containing trees over three hundred years old can still be seen on undisturbed sites. Hardwood forests are uncommon, but do occur on the well-drained glacial hills.

Many bird species such as pileated woodpecker, barred owl, chickadee and red-eyed vireo make these woods their home along with a few rare species like the scarlet tanager and great-crested flycatcher.

In addition, mammals like the white-tailed deer, black bear and bobcat occur in varied habitats throughout the park.

Wetlands of several types are found here. Large, treeless bogs often bordering lakes are so wet that growth is limited to water-tolerant plants like sphagnum moss, leather leaf and pitcher plant. Black spruce and tamarack forests are found on drier bogs.

Waterways are the essence of Kejimkujik. Kejimkujik Lake is one of the largest in the province, providing an unequalled canoeing experience. In calm weather the hidden coves and islands offer hours of paddling enjoyment.

Most park waters are dark brown in colour, stained by the bogs through which they flow. A few lakes, such as Beaverskin and Mountain, are clear, fed by springs and runoff from the surrounding land.

Yellow and white perch inhabit all waterways, while many have good populations of brook trout. Beaver, mink and otter inhabit lakes and rivers throughout the park.

Cape Breton Highlands National Park, Nova Scotia

Cape Breton Highlands was created in 1936 and became the first national park in the Atlantic Provinces. Located in the northern portion of Cape Breton Island it covers 950 square kilometres, bounded on the west by the Gulf of St. Lawrence and on the east by the Atlantic Ocean.

The area was first inhabited by Micmac Indians who probably were the first to see John Cabot touch North America in 1497 at Aspy Bay, just north of the park. Portuguese fishermen settled in the vicinity of Ingonish in the 1520's. They were followed by the French who occupied Cape Breton Island (then known as "Isle Royale") during most of the 17th Century. Ingonish, or "Port d'Orleans" as it was known then, was the second largest centre on the island. Louisbourg, which is now a National Historic Park, was at that time the most important centre in the French colony. After its destruction by the British most of the French settlements including "Port d'Orleans" were abandoned. The expulsion of the Acadians from mainland Nova Scotia in the mid 1700's led to the establishment of French settlements along Cape Breton's western shore. Many of these remain today.

The 19th Century brought a major influx of English, Irish and Scottish settlers whose descendants now inhabit most of the Island.

The park's main feature is an extensive plateau which covers ninety percent of the area. Some 360 metres above sea level, most of the plateau is covered with extensive bogs, dry barrens, small ponds and lakes. The Cabot Trail encircles the plateau, offering spectacular glimpses of some of the last remaining wilderness in Nova Scotia.

Rivers and streams have cut deep valleys into the tableland, leaving picturesque waterfalls where stubborn rock has failed to give way. Along the coast, bold headlands, steep cliffs, hidden coves and beaches are products of the relentless pounding of the sea.

The plateau supports a variety of vegetation, from plants normally found in Canada's far north to heath plants on the bogs and stunted balsam fir and black spruce on the dryer crests. Rich mixed hardwoods such as sugar maple, yellow birch and beech, are found in the more temperate river valleys while white spruce is the most predominant species found on the coastal slopes. Numerous lichens and mosses as well as countless varieties of wildflowers and shrubs all help to make Cape Breton Highlands National Park rich in plant life.

The animal life of the lowlands is largely typical of eastern Canada with species such as moose, white-tailed deer, black bear, snowshoe hare, bob cat and fox. The highlands are home to small populations of pine marten, lynx and possibly cougar. Bird life is extensive with up to 230 species on the list of sightings in and around the park. Eastern brook trout can be found in most of the park lakes and streams and a number of rivers also play host to the annual Atlantic salmon spawning run. A full range of salt water fishes and mammals, such as pilot whales and seals, may be seen offshore.

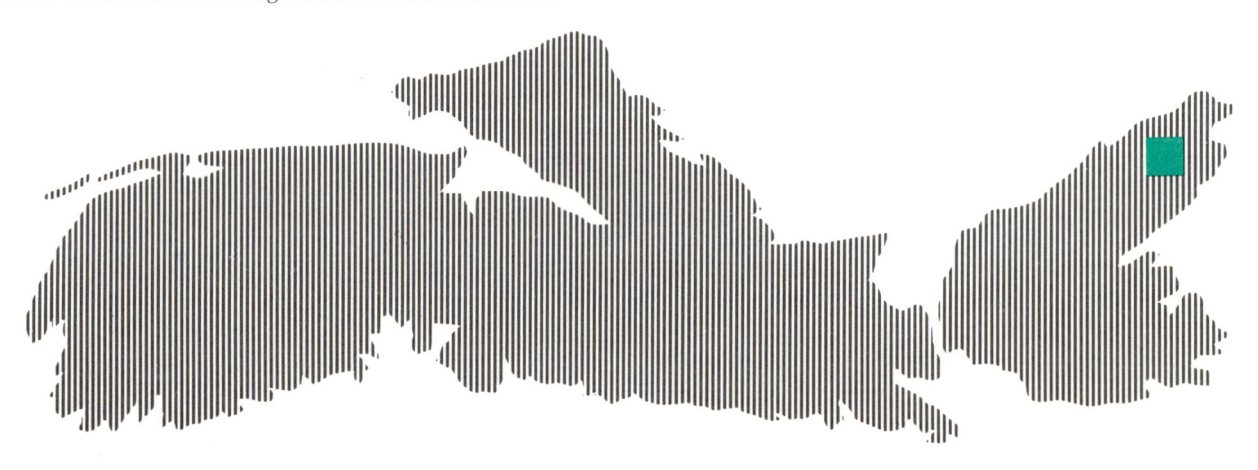

Ingonish Beach and Cape Smokey, Cape Breton Highlands National Park

Prince Edward Island National Park

Prince Edward Island National Park is a narrow coastal area of thirty-two square kilometres, along the Gulf of St. Lawrence, encompassing a varied landscape of sand dunes, red sandstone cliffs, marshes, ponds and some of the finest salt-water beaches in Canada.

The first European settlers arrived in the park area in 1770, and, as late as the 1930's, many of their descendants still farmed the land. The old dykes and flat forest floor are reminders of fields farmed long before the park was established in 1937.

Not only were the people dependent on the land, they also looked to the sea for their livelihood. For generations people have fished from these shores and more recently, harvesting Irish moss has become an important industry. Boatbuilding was also a thriving activity during the 19th Century.

In the latter part of the 1800's, the area's fine beaches had already begun to attract large numbers of summer visitors and tourist facilities were being developed. Shaw's Hotel and Stanhope Beach Inn were among the first hotels to accommodate visitors and these two establishments are still operating just outside the Park today. Green Gables House is located at the far western end of the Park in Cavendish. This charming farmhouse is known internationally through Lucy Maud Montgomery's classic novel "Anne of Green Gables" as the house where Anne lived.

Prince Edward Island was formed by an accumulation of sand and mud deposited in a large ocean basin. Over millenia, continuing accumulation resulted in the formation of sandstone which is the base of the island. A characteristic of sandstone is that it can be easily broken apart. Evidence of this can be seen in the park where the red sandstone cliffs are continually being eroded by the action of waves.

The formation of the park's famous beaches is a complicated but fascinating story. The sandstone rubble that accumulates at the base of the cliffs is broken down into sand grains and is transported offshore and along the shore by waves and currents. Some of the sand then accumulates offshore resulting in the development of sand bars, eventually forming barrier islands. Although only hundreds of meters in width, often these islands are several kilometres long.

Under the influence of storm waves and winds, these barrier islands then migrate shoreward depositing large quantities of sand along the shore resulting in the extensive beaches seen today. The beach sand is then driven further onshore by wind action and trapped by marram grass; this results in the formation of coastal dunes.

Spit formation, associated with coastal sand movement, may also transform bays into landlocked ponds. These ponds provide habitats for the many birds that nest here in the summer as well as the other plants and animals that require these fresh water environments to survive.

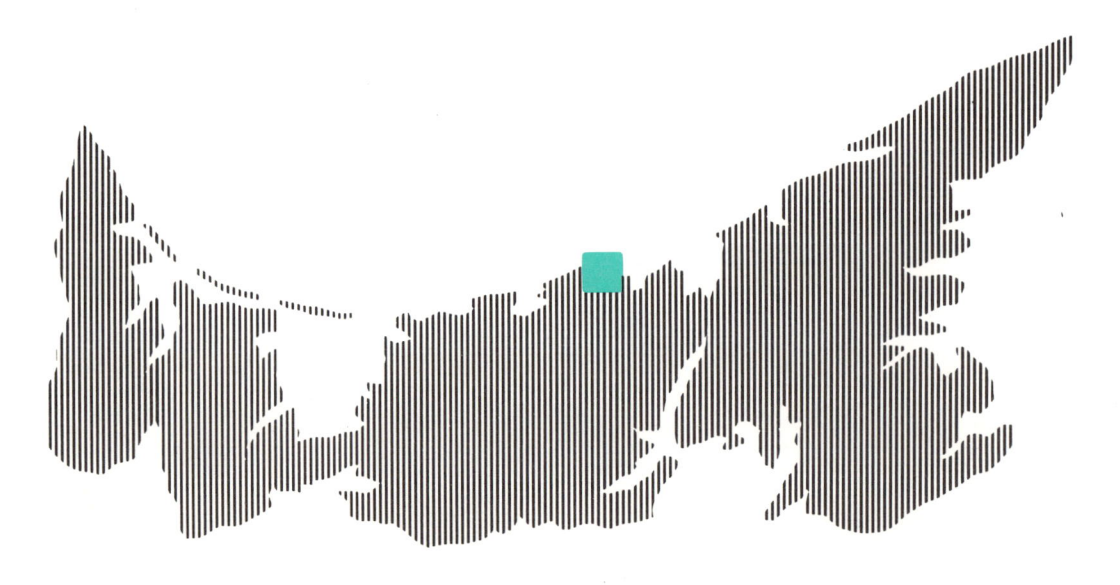

Cavendish Beach, Prince Edward Island National Park

Gros Morne National Park, Newfoundland

Gros Morne National Park, created in 1970, is located on the west coast of Newfoundland's Great Northern Peninsula. It contains some of Canada's most geologically interesting and visually spectacular land forms. Eons ago, the Long Range Mountains were formed. Since then, erosion and the grinding of glaciers from the ice age have sculpted and shaped them into their present form. These two agents of nature have created such features as the fjord-like ponds of Western Brook, Baker's Brook and St. Paul's Inlet and the tableland on the south side of Bonne Bay. The land gradually rose from the sea, and is in fact still rising, to form the coastal plain which lies between the sea and the mountains.

The park area, rich in human history, had three pre-European cultures living within its boundaries. The Maritime Archaic Indians were present between 2500 B.C. and 1000 B.C. Artifacts, including harpoons, indicate that these people lived mainly on marine mammals and caribou. Their carvings show the respect given to larger mammals such as the killer whale.

Evidence of the Dorset Eskimo culture, which flourished between 100 and 700 A.D., is found along the coastline as far south as Norris Point. The Dorset Eskimos, like the Maritime Archaic Indians, lived on sea and land animals. Artifacts from their time show an advanced culture capable of using such implements as knife blades, projectile points, harpoons and sled runners.

The Beothuck Indians, the third of these cultures, inhabited Gros Morne from about 800 A.D. In summer they lived on the coast, harvesting the sea, while during the winter they moved inland in pursuit of the caribou herds. The Beothucks became extinct in 1829 with the death of Shanadithit, the last member of this race.

In 1534 Jacques Cartier was the first European to visit the area when he put into a small cove near Cow Head for protection from a storm. Colonization followed soon after with small fishing villages appearing along the coast. Today fishermen still make their living from the sea much as their forefathers did.

Gros Morne National Park possesses a complex and diverse plant community due to its location on the Gulf of St. Lawrence, its varied types of bedrock and soil and its large range of elevation. Wherever the coastline faces the open sea, there is a narrow zone of windshaped and stunted balsam fir and white spruce. This growth form is known technically as Krummholz and locally as "tuckamore".

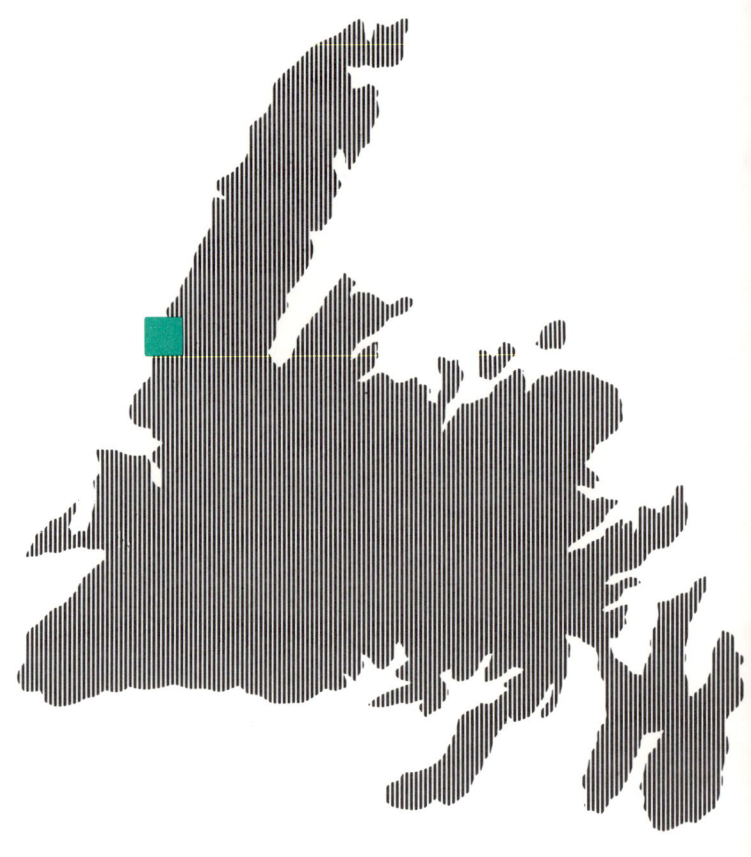

The flat terrain of the coastal plain is mostly covered with bogs. Sphagnum mosses and insect-capturing plants such as the pitcher plant are especially adapted for survival in this environment. The meandering brooks of the lowlands are bordered by alder swales.

The drier lowland slopes have been extensively logged and in many places there is a dense second growth of balsam fir and white birch. The wind-exposed morainic ridges and mountain slopes support shrub-like heath vegetation, stunted black spruce and mountain alder.

Because of its elevation and exposure to drying winds, the top of the Long Range plateau has tundra-like vegetation interspersed with rock barrens. Mosses form conspicuous cushion-like mats between protecting rocks.

The moose and snowshoe hare, although not native to Newfoundland, are two of the more noteworthy park mammals. Large native mammals such as the caribou, black bear and lynx are found mainly in remote wilderness areas of Gros Morne. Beaver are gradually increasing in number and can be observed in many streams and ponds.

Birds are much more varied in Gros Morne National Park than are mammals. Common and arctic terns, herring gulls and great black-backed gulls are characteristic of the sea coast while willow and rock ptarmigan typify the bird life of the heath-lands and barrens.

Western Brook Pond, Gros Morne National Park

Terra Nova National Park, Newfoundland

Since its establishment in 1957, Terra Nova National Park has protected remnants of the ancient Appalachian Mountains. Rocky headlands provide shelter from the awesome power of the open ocean.

The region owes its temperate climate to the influence of the sea. The warm Gulf Stream flowing past the Island of Newfoundland delays and moderates the onset of winter, while the cold force of the Labrador Current lends a chill to the spring and early summer months. This Arctic current brings with it pack-ice and enormous icebergs from the glaciers of Greenland and the polar cap.

In turn, the moderate climate of Terra Nova affects the area's plants and animals. Rolling hills are cloaked in the greens and greys of black spruce and balsam fir. Wetlands are rich in low-lying vegetation such as mosses, orchids and the insect-eating pitcher plant.

Because the ocean isolates Newfoundland from the mainland, the wildlife of Terra Nova differs from other boreal forests. There are no porcupines, skunks, or snakes. Many introduced mammals, including snowshoe hare and moose, are now as plentiful as the native lynx, bear and beaver.

The coastal region of Terra Nova National Park varies from the rugged cliffs of Mount Stamford to the gentle, sandy beach at Cobbler's Day Use Area. Sea urchins, starfish, mussels, periwinkles and rock crabs survive along the rocky coast. In the Newman Sound area, marine worms, clams and tiny crustaceans flourish in the mudflats. You may see bald eagles, ospreys, ducks and shorebirds feeding here. Further from shore, whales and dolphins are attracted by the presence of squid and caplin.

Most reminders of Terra Nova's cultural heritage lie along the coast. Over 2000 years ago, the earliest inhabitants, the Maritime Archaic Indians, took their food from the ocean in summer and from the land in winter. The Dorset Eskimos followed, and later the Beothucks, or "red Indians", so named for their tradition of painting their bodies with red ochre.

Europeans reached Terra Nova as early as the 1500's. Explorers, fishermen and pirates travelled this coast, taking refuge and settling in the many hidden coves and harbours.

Fishing was a major industry, and despite challenging conditions and nearly total isolation, people stayed and settled along the coast. By the mid-1600's, British settlers had established scattered communities throughout the area now called Terra Nova National Park. In time, logging, shipbuilding and agriculture became important activities.

Many local people still follow this tradition, fishing in summer, and in winter harvesting wood for fuel and building materials from the forests surrounding the park.

Blue Hills, Terra Nova National Park

TABLE 1				NATIONAL PARKS		
MAP REF.	NAME	GRID/LOCATION		YEAR EST.	SIZE (SQ. KMS)	NATURAL REGION
1	Kouchibouguac	D5	Gulf of St. Lawrence, New Brunswick	1969	238.0	32: Maritime Plain
2	Fundy	C5	Fundy Shore, New Brunswick	1948	205.9	31: Maritime Acadian Highlands
3	Kejimkujik	B4	Southwestern Nova Scotia	1968	381.5	33: Atlantic Coast Uplands
4	Cape Breton Highlands	D9	Cape Breton, Nova Scotia	1936	950.5	31: Maritime Acadian Highlands
5	Prince Edward Island	D6	North Shore, Prince Edward Island	1937	32.0	32: Maritime Plain
6	Gros Morne	G12	Western Newfoundland	1970	1,942.5	34: Western Newfoundland Highlands
7	Terra Nova	F15	Northeast Newfoundland	1957	396.5	35: Eastern Newfoundland Island
	TOTAL (7)				4,146.9	

Deer Island Archipelago

Natural Areas of Canadian Significance

As part of its park system planning process, Parks Canada identifies natural areas which encompass a great variety of natural features and which are considered to be representative of the natural region in which they are situated. These areas are referred to as "Natural Areas of Canadian Significance".

In order to complete the national park system, at least one such area should be included from each of the thirty-nine terrestrial and twenty-nine marine natural regions of Canada. Although the Atlantic Region is well represented, at present the overall terrestrial system is only about half completed, and there are no national marine parks yet established.

While Parks Canada conducts systematic studies of marine and terrestrial natural regions, which result in the identification of many representative and unique natural areas, suggestions are also welcomed from informed individuals or groups. While these areas have no current legal status whatsoever, some of them may in future receive protection under the National Parks Act in order to fill the voids in the national park system. However, Parks Canada cannot protect all of those natural areas identified as being of Canadian significance. By establishing and making public a register that lists all of the identified areas, Parks Canada hopes to encourage other organizations to share responsibility for their protection.

In Atlantic Canada, there are seven areas which have been identified as natural areas of Canadian significance.

Deer Island Archipelago, New Brunswick

This island archipelago is located close to the New Brunswick shore near the mouth of the Bay of Fundy. It consists of some forty islands, and numerous reefs, shoals, passages and ledges. The coastline is rugged and rocky and presents some of the finest maritime scenery in the Bay of Fundy. Local mixing and upwelling of the cold

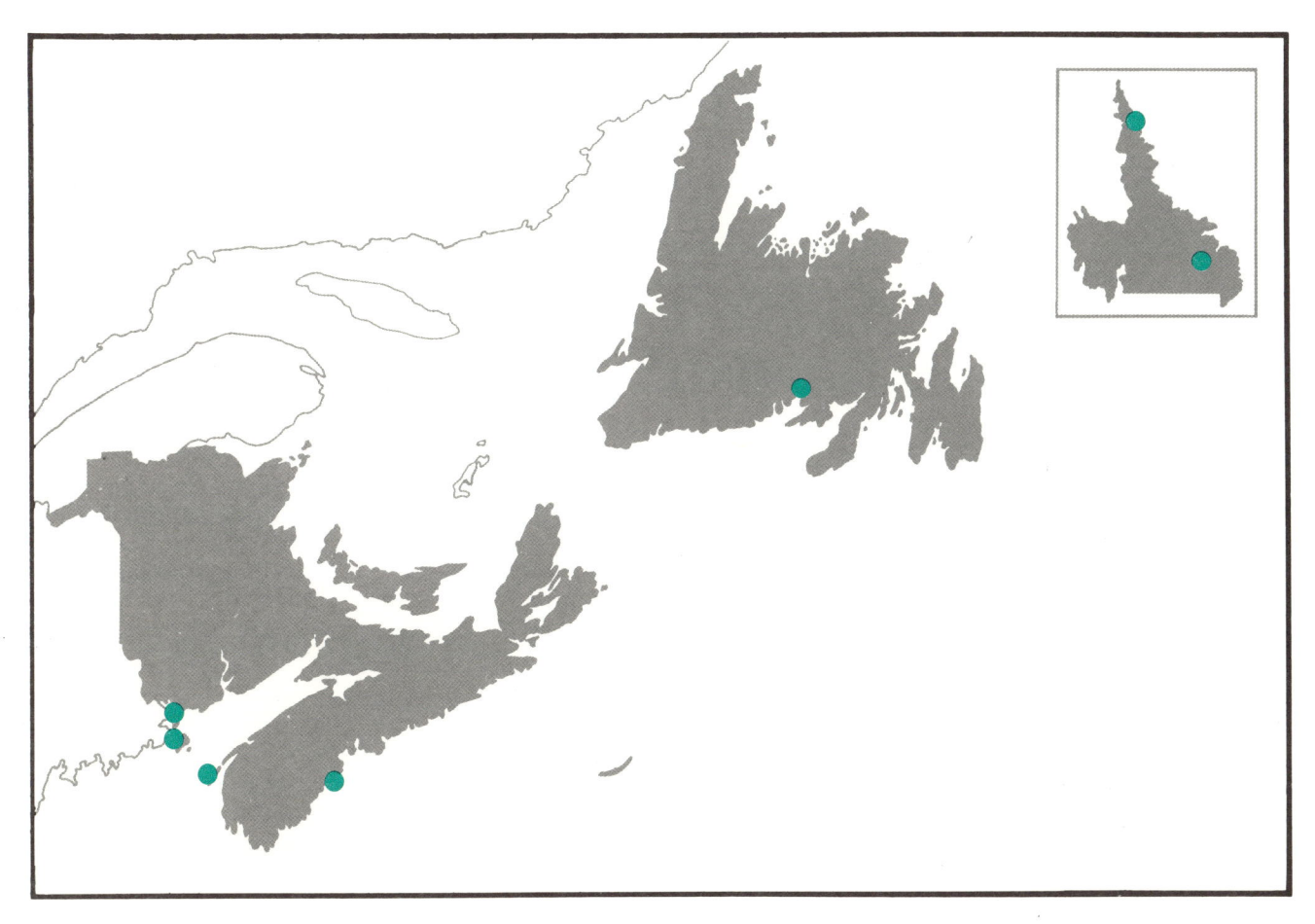

25

saline waters contributes to an abundance of zooplankton, the foundation of the marine biological food chain in the western Bay of Fundy.

The islands, islets, and channels support seabird breeding colonies as well as feeding areas for vast populations of migrating and wintering waterfowl and shorebirds. Major breeding colonies of black guillemots, great and double-crested cormorants, eider ducks, herring and great black-backed gulls are scattered throughout the archipelago. The endangered right and humpback whales, as well as finback and minke whales, are regular visitors to the area. Large numbers of harbour seals and harbour porpoise also inhabit these waters.

The significance of this area as a marine nursery and rearing area for marine flora and fauna has been recognized by the scientific community. The archipelago is one of the most outstanding regions for observing marine life in the Bay of Fundy.

Grand Manan Archipelago, New Brunswick

The Grand Manan Archipelago is adjacent to Deer Island in the Bay of Fundy. It consists of some fifteen major islands, numerous islets, ledges, shoals, reefs, and tidal flats. A moderate maritime climate subjects the archipelago to periods of prolonged fog and inclement weather.

The shallow waters provide a suitable habitat for the rich and abundant marine life characteristic of the outer Bay of Fundy, Atlantic and Virginian faunal provinces.

Southwest Head, Grand Manan Island

The Island is a key staging area for migrating shorebirds and waterfowl. Critical nesting habitats for black guillemots, Leach's storm petrels, black-crowned night heron, herring and great black-backed gulls are located on the various islands. A significant number of grey and harbour seals along with fin, minke, humpback and right whales, harbour porpoises, white-sided dolphins feed in the waters around Grand Manan.

Coastal geology is characterized by spectacular basalt cliffs. The osprey and bald eagle nest on these cliffs and bluffs throughout the Archipelago.

The Archipelago is rich in coastal marine history. Historic shipwrecks abound throughout the many passages and shoals.

Brier Island, Nova Scotia

Brier Island, at the tip of Digby Neck, and its adjacent marine area is biologically, one of the richest areas in the Bay of Fundy Marine Region. The island has a moderate marine climate with extensive summer fogs. The highest mean January temperatures and mildest extreme low temperatures in the Maritimes occur here.

Highly saline marine waters support an abundance of zooplankton and fish. This vital feeding area supports migrant seabirds, exceptional in numbers of individuals and species. A significant number and diversity of seals and whales feed and winter in these marine waters. The subtidal and intertidal marine flora and fauna are unusually rich and contains southern (Virginian) species which are rare or absent elsewhere in the Maritimes.

Steep cliffs and surf swept rocks of columnar basalts characterize the coast. Extensive and relatively undisturbed shoreland bogs support floral and faunal species which are unique in Atlantic Canada.

The area is outstanding for observation of birds of the Atlantic flyway, as it attracts the most diverse group of migrant land and shorebirds in the Bay of Fundy Marine Region. Shoreland ponds attract migrant and over-wintering waterfowl.

Cape La Have Islands, Nova Scotia

The Cape La Have Islands and mainland fringe are representative of the irregular and diverse coastline of south-western Nova Scotia. The area also provides a representative sample of Atlantic coastal beaches ranging from fine sand to shingle beach and varying in character from sheltered beaches such as Risser's to the surf-swept beaches of Bantan Bay and King Beach. The three major marine environments of the Nova Scotia coast and their inhabitants are present in the area: the warm brackish waters of the protected bays and estuaries containing temperate and boreal species; the exposed outer beaches and semi-protected rocky shores with their boreal species; and the cold water reefs with their sub-arctic species.

The mainland area behind the beaches is typical of a glaciated area and is characterized by a series of drumlins providing scenic views of the Atlantic Ocean. A number of terrestrial and coastal ecosystems occur such as the coastal white spruce forest, salt and fresh water wetlands, dunes and beaches, salt marshes, pioneer plant ecosystems tolerant of wind and spray, estuary ecosystems and sea bird colonies.

Baie d'Espoir, Newfoundland

The isolated Baie d'Espoir area on Newfoundland's south coast is dominated by a high, barren coastal upland which is indented by several long, deep fjords, some of which exceed 250 metres in depth. Central Baie d'Espoir itself reaches a depth in excess of 755 metres within five kilometres of shore, and provides a unique, inshore field laboratory for the scientific investigation of the oceanography and biology of deep ocean waters. The coastal relief of the area is spectacular, encompassing long, narrow fjords, high cliff walls and promontories with names such as Blow Me Down, Ironskull, Sugar Loaf and the Highland of La Hune. Numerous waterfalls and abundant evidence of a glacial past, including hanging valleys, cirques, and scoured slopes all contribute to the diversity of the area.

In marked contrast to the three marine natural areas of Canadian significance in the Bay of Fundy, the Baie d'Espoir area has low tidal amplitude, weak currents, little upwelling and biological productivity is relatively low. Nevertheless, there are resident populations of herring and greater black-backed gulls, arctic terns, cormorants, black guillemots and other seabirds. The concentration of bald eagles is reputed to be the highest in eastern Canada. There is a stable inshore fishery for cod and other groundfish and pelagic species, sufficient to support three remote outports. Of particular note is that many of the eastern Canadian records of fish species such as blue ling, deepsea angler, and Atlantic soft pout are from the deep waters close to the Hermitage Channel. Humpback, blue, finback and minke whales are frequent visitors, as are pilot whales, white-sided dolphins, and harbour porpoises. A small population of harbour seals is resident in the northern arm of Baie d'Espoir.

Mealy Mountains

Mealy Mountains, Labrador

The Mealy Mountains area contains excellent examples of the four physiographic components that represent the East Coast Boreal Region's natural character. From the marine environment along the southern shore of Lake Melville, the area rises gradually through the coastal plain, then abruptly to an extensive rugged plateau interlaced with numerous ponds and narrow, elongated lakes. These three components finally culminate in 1,100 metre peaks along the eastern boundary.

The coastal plain, plateau and adjacent mountain systems possess surficial features such as spectacular waterfalls and rivers, elongated trough lakes, cirques and tarns which are vivid evidence of past glaciation. Throughout the area two diverse plant communities have developed: one representing the tundra ecosystem, the other the boreal forest. As a result, there is a variety of fauna including a resident population of caribou, moose, black bear, beaver, fox, otter, mink and many species of birds. The marine environment also provides a favourable habitat for many seabirds.

Torngat Mountains, Labrador

The Torngat Mountains form the highest and the most rugged peaks of eastern mainland Canada. Elevations over 1,500 metres are common and recent glaciation has left deeply incised valleys and a rugged fjordal coastline. In addition, the area contains excellent representations of coastal plains, plateaus, lakes, islands, braided river systems, and glacial and periglacial landforms.

This area lies north of the treeline within the Arctic tundra ecosystem and displays a diversity of plants and animals. The valleys support migrating herds of caribou, black bears, foxes and other mammals, while whales, seals and other marine mammals are frequently seen offshore. Many species of birds (Canada goose, harlequin duck, common eider, rough-legged hawk, gryfalcon, arctic tern) nest in the area during the summer months.

Climatic conditions are severe. Constant winds sweep the area, frequently reaching gale force. Cool temperatures are prevalent during the short growing season.

The area offers an excellent representation of the natural themes to be found in the Northern Labrador Mountains Natural Region.

Torngat Mountains

TABLE 2		NATURAL AREAS OF CANADIAN SIGNIFICANCE	
MAP REF.	NAME	GRID/LOCATION	NATURAL REGION
8	Deer Island Archipelago	B3 Bay of Fundy, New Brunswick	Bay of Fundy Marine Region
9	Grand Manan Archipelago	B3 Bay of Fundy, New Brunswick	Bay of Fundy Marine Region
10	Brier Island	B3 Digby Neck, Nova Scotia	Bay of Fundy Marine Region
11	Cape La Have Islands	B5 South Shore, Nova Scotia	33: Atlantic Coast Uplands
12	Baie d'Espoir	E14 South Shore, Newfoundland	Laurentian Trough Marine Region
13	Mealy Mountains	X3 Southern Labrador	21: East Coast Boreal Region
14	Torngat Mountains	Y2 Northern Labrador	24: Northern Labrador Mountains
	TOTAL (7)		

Canadian Heritage Rivers

Since 1971, Parks Canada has been pursuing an initiative that is just now beginning to come to fruition. The Wild Rivers Survey, conducted from 1971 to 1973, gathered information on approximately 16,650 kilometres of rivers across Canada. The survey provided an opportunity for analyzing and comparing the scenic and recreational resources of major Canadian heritage rivers, and provided an opportunity to formulate goals for the preservation of the best examples of these rivers and their associated lands.

Subsequently, Parks Canada undertook a series of consultations with provincial and territorial governments to determine the most appropriate means of protection. In 1978, federal, provincial and territorial parks' ministers asked their officials to work together to prepare a joint proposal for a Canadian Heritage Rivers System. A task force was set up and in July, 1981, it published a report with the recommendation that the system should be a cooperative one in which participating governments would retain their traditional jurisdictional powers. These powers include the ownership of land, the choice to nominate a river to the system and the right to continue to operate and manage designated rivers in accordance with the objectives of the system.

The formal establishment of the Canadian Heritage Rivers System was announced on January 18, 1984. In the Atlantic Region, New Brunswick, Newfoundland and Nova Scotia have agreed to participate.

A Canadian Heritage Rivers Board has been established, comprised of members appointed by the federal government and each of the provincial and territorial governments choosing to participate. The Board's primary function is to review nominations by the appropriate managing jurisdictions and to recommend to the Ministers responsible for Parks Canada and the nominating agency(ies) concerned, formal designation of each river that meets the guidelines for selection.

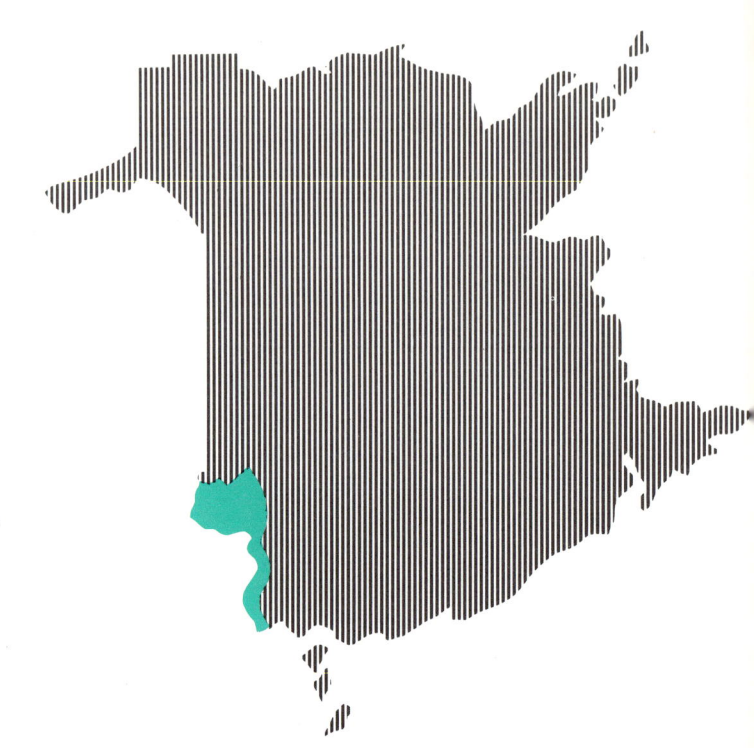

So far, in the Atlantic Region, only the St. Croix River in New Brunswick has been submitted to the Board and accepted as a candidate heritage river, pending completion of a management plan which must be lodged with the Board within three years of nomination. A number of other rivers are currently being considered by the other participating provinces.

TABLE 3		CANADIAN HERITAGE RIVERS	
MAP REF.	NAME	GRID/LOCATION	FEATURES
15	St. Croix River	C2 Southwestern New Brunswick	Novice, white water canoeing, outdoor recreation, nature observation

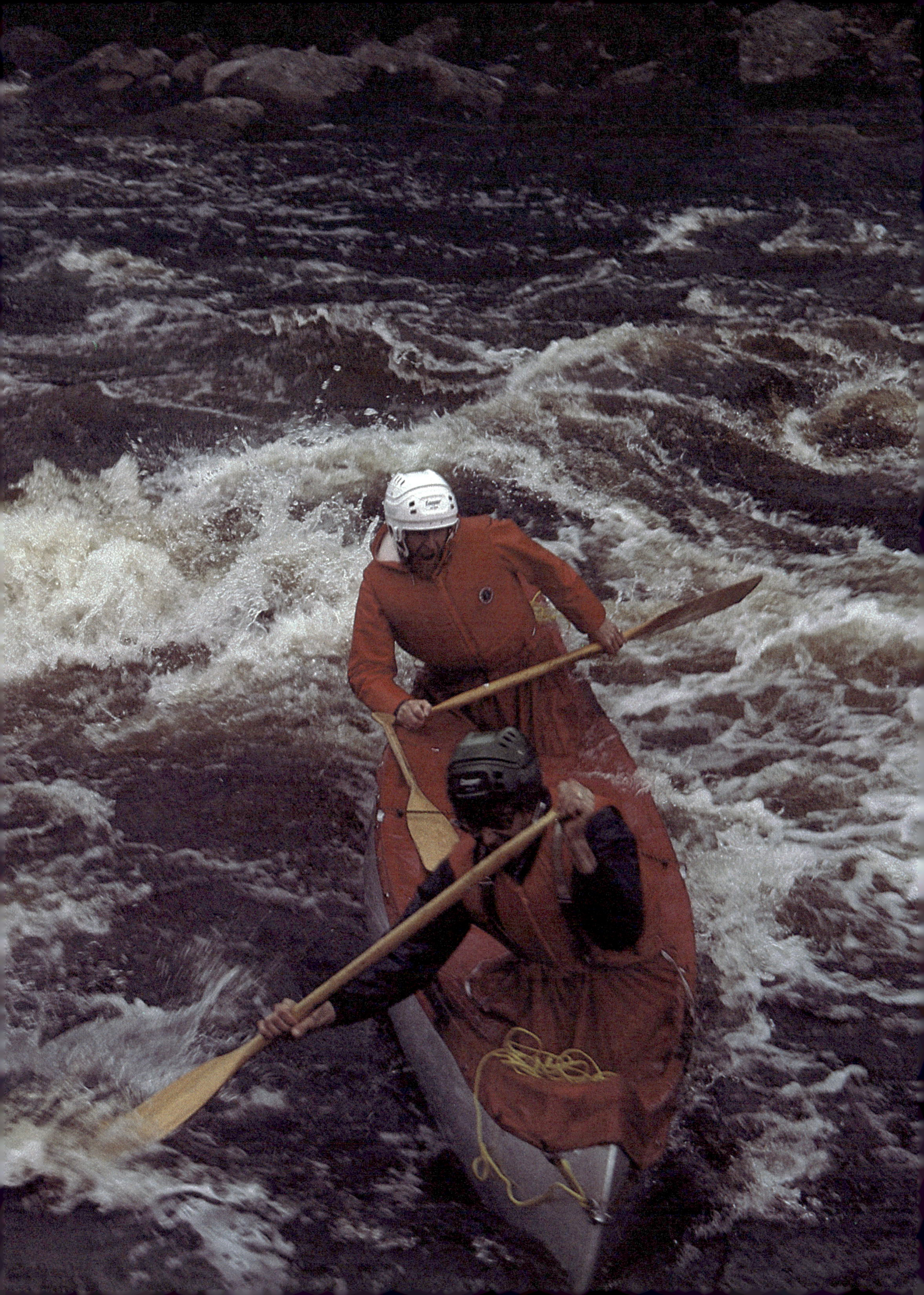

National Wildlife Areas

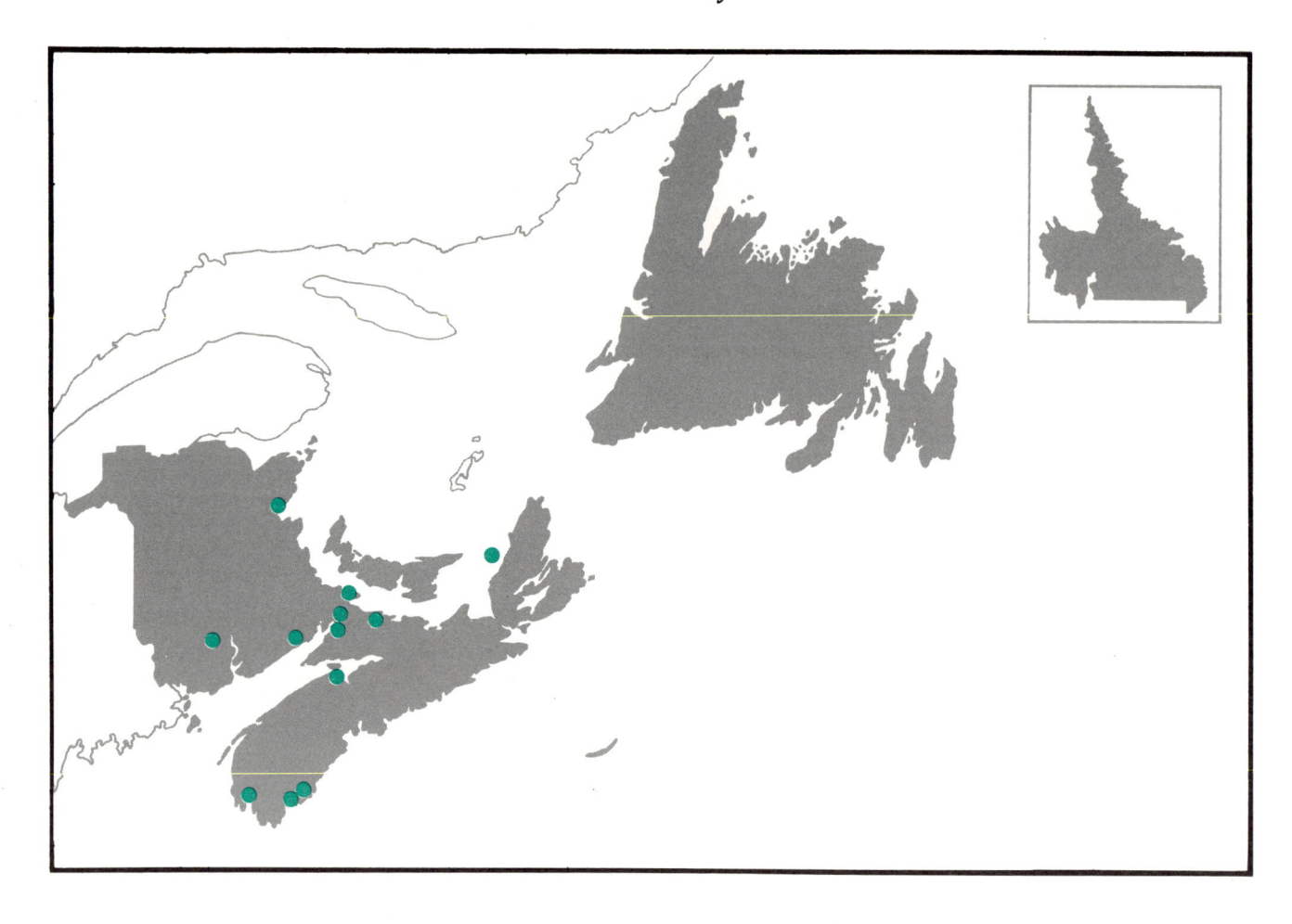

National Wildlife Areas are owned and managed by the Canadian Wildlife Service on behalf of the federal government. The national wildlife area program began in 1966 when a policy statement was tabled in the House of Commons by the then Minister responsible for the Canadian Wildlife Service. This policy identified the importance of protecting habitat for wildlife and set out provisions whereby land was to be acquired for this purpose. CWS in the Atlantic Region began its program of land acquisition by acquiring Sand Pond in Yarmouth County, Nova Scotia in 1967, and several other areas soon thereafter. The Canada Wildlife Act was passed in 1973, but lands could not be formally declared until they were scheduled under the National Wildlife Area Regulations which were adopted in 1977.

Currently there are twelve national wildlife areas in the Atlantic Region, seven in Nova Scotia and five in New Brunswick.

Portage Island National Wildlife Area, New Brunswick

Portage Island National Wildlife Area is located in Miramichi Bay, thirty-eight kilometres northwest of Chatham, Northumberland County. The island consists entirely of a series of coastal barrier beaches, alternating sand ridges and slacks. The ridges are vegetated by dune communities with a progression from marram grass to lichen — shrub forest. The dune slacks on the east side of the island and the fringe bordering the island's sheltered bay are vegetated by salt marsh. Brackish marshes and swamps occupy interior slacks. Extensive sand-gravel beaches surround the island. The island is a candidate ecological reserve site.

The shallow waters around Portage Island National Wildlife Area and its sheltered bay provide staging and migration habitat for waterfowl. The dune slacks and interior ponds afford a limited amount of waterfowl production habitat. Its sand beaches and flats are used by migrating shorebirds. Ospreys nest on the island. Waterfowl hunting, subject to provincial and federal regulations, is permitted. Wildlife observation, hiking and the picking of wild berries are also permitted.

Portobello Creek National Wildlife Area, New Brunswick

The area is part of a large alluvial flat located thirty-two kilometres east of Fredericton, New Brunswick, adjacent to the Saint John River. Each spring, when the river overflows its banks, all but the highest forested sites are completely submerged. It is a unique flood-plain system with Portobello Creek following a meandering course through large expanses of open marsh, shrub swamp, wooded swale and forest.

The Portobello Creek area provides important production, staging and migration habitat for waterfowl. It is one of the most naturally productive sites in the Atlantic provinces and in addition to the more common waterfowl species, it is one of the few locations hosting significant breeding populations of tree-nesting birds. The flood-plain forest and adjoining wooded uplands afford habitat for a variety of songbirds and large mammals such as moose, white-tailed deer and black bear. The area has been identified as a candidate ecological reserve by the provincial government.

Hunting, trapping, fishing, canoeing and wildlife observation are all important activities undertaken in the area.

Beaver Lodge, Portobello Creek National Wildlife Area

Shepody National Wildlife Area, New Brunswick

Shepody National Wildlife Area is comprised of the Germantown Marsh, Mary's Point and New Horton sections. They are situated on and adjacent to Chignecto Bay, forty kilometres south of Moncton. Both the Germantown marsh and New Horton sections were largely former salt marshes that had been converted to farmland with the installation of dikes and a bideau that held back the tidal waters. Since being incorporated into the Shepody National Wildlife Area these marshes have been impounded by Ducks Unlimited with earth dikes and shallowly flooded with fresh water.

The Mary's Point section is situated on the coast where Shepody and Chignecto Bay converge, and is comprised of a large salt marsh, extensive intertidal mud flats and a forested peninsula that extends out into Shepody Bay.

The salt marshes and impounded wetlands of Shepody National Wildlife Area provide important production, staging and migration habitat for waterfowl and nesting habitat for a variety of marshbirds and waterfowl. The intertidal mud flats and gravel beaches of Mary's Point provide one of the most important migration sites in North America.

Waterfowl hunting and trapping are major activities on the Germantown and New Horton marsh sections. Wildlife observation, particularly of the autumn shorebird flocks, is the most important activity at the Mary's Point section.

Marsh Hawk

Tintamarre National Wildlife Area, New Brunswick

Tintamarre National Wildlife Area lies along the upper fringe of the reclaimed Tantramar Marshes, ten kilometres northeast of Sackville, Westmoreland County. It is comprised of a series of shallow lake basins which are surrounded by extensive wetlands ranging from fens and swamp to treed bogs. Portions of the wetlands, as well as sections of reclaimed tidal marsh, have been converted to shallow impoundments which comprise fifteen percent of the area. Also included in the wildlife area are smaller tracts of forested and cultivated upland. A large bog within the area has been identified as candidate ecological reserve by the province of New Brunswick.

Tintamarre National Wildlife Area provides production and staging habitat for several species of waterfowl. Habitat management has resulted in significant increases in waterfowl production. The shallowly-flooded impoundments afford nesting habitat for a variety of marsh birds and good muskrat habitat. Marsh hawks nest commonly in the area, and the uplands provide nesting habitat for songbirds. This site has been used extensively for wetland research projects.

Fishing, hunting and trapping are permitted subject to provincial and federal regulations. Wildlife observation, canoeing, hiking, skiing and berry-picking are also permitted.

Tintamarre National Wildlife Area

Cape Jourimain National Wildlife Area, New Brunswick

Cape Jourimain National Wildlife Area is a coastal site located eight kilometres northwest of Cape Tormentine. It consists of an association of salt marshes, brackish marshes, fresh water wetlands, barrier beach, sand dune and upland. The Cape itself is comprised of two islands (Inner and Outer Jourimain Islands), and the marshes that connect them to the adjoining upland. A road was built across the area in the 1960's providing a more substantial link between the islands and the mainland. The road, which was formerly the approach to a proposed causeway between New Brunswick and Prince Edward Island, remains today despite the abandonment of the causeway endeavor. Besides providing greater access, the road has had a pronounced effect on the landscape in that it blocked the normal tidal flow into a portion of the marsh which resulted in the formation of two large brackish ponds. Although not by design, this has increased the value of the area for wildlife.

Cape Jourimain is frequented by large numbers of migrant waterfowl and provides nesting and rearing habitat for several waterfowl species. It attracts a large and very diversified group of shorebirds and in that regard is one of the most exceptional areas in the Atlantic region.

Fishing, hunting and trapping are permitted (subject to provincial and federal regulations) on all of the area except a small section adjacent to the community of Bayfield. Wildlife observation, canoeing, hiking and the picking of wild berries and greens are permitted on the entire area. All other activities are prohibited unless a permit has been obtained from the Canadian Wildlife Service.

Canadian Lynx

Chignecto National Wildlife Area, Nova Scotia

Chignecto National Wildlife Area is located five kilometres southwest of Amherst, Cumberland County, Nova Scotia.

It is comprised of the John Lusby saltmarsh section and the Amherst Point sanctuary section. The John Lusby section consists of an extensive tract of saltmarsh bordering on the Cumberland Basin. The Amherst Point sanctuary is a mosaic of ponds, freshwater marshes, bogs, forests and old farm fields. A large portion of the sanctuary's wetlands has been improved for wildlife by Ducks Unlimited through the construction of dikes and control structures. Two small impoundments have also been developed next to the upland on the John Lusby section. The two sections of Chignecto National Wildlife Area are separated by the narrow Amherst Point ridge.

The John Lusby saltmarsh is particularly important to Canada geese migrating north in the spring. It is also used extensively by other waterfowl during the spring and fall migrations and the late summer staging periods. The Amherst Point sanctuary provides a migration and staging habitat and is an important waterfowl production site. Several waterfowl species having limited distribution and uncommon occurrence in the region breed at Amherst Point. Its diverse wetland and upland habitat affords an important nesting and migration habitat for several marshbird and tree-nesting species.

Waterfowl hunting is permitted on the John Lusby saltmarsh. On the Amherst Point sanctuary, where hunting is prohibited, the public can enjoy a variety of activities including wildlife observation, photography, nature education and walking. Muskrat trapping and fishing are also permitted.

Chignecto National Wildlife Area

Wallace Bay National Wildlife Area, Nova Scotia

Wallace Bay National Wildlife Area is situated at the upper limit of Wallace Harbour on the Northumberland Strait, eight kilometres east of Pugwash, Cumberland County, Nova Scotia. It is comprised of marine and freshwater wetlands, forested uplands and fields. A road and bideau across the area divide the wetlands almost equally into marine and freshwater. The marine wetland is comprised of tidal channels and saltmarsh. A section of the saltmarsh area has been impounded creating a shallow brackish wetland. Impounded wetlands have also been developed over a large section of the freshwater marsh.

Wallace Bay National Wildlife Area provides migration and production habitat for waterfowl. Habitat management has resulted in significant increases in waterfowl production. The shallow wetlands also afford nesting habitat for several species of marshbirds. Several other bird species also frequent the wetlands and many nest in the surrounding uplands. Muskrat are particularly abundant and many other mammal species inhabit the wildlife area. A pair of bald eagles currently nest on the site.

Fishing, hunting and trapping are permitted subject to provincial and federal regulations. Wildlife observation, canoeing, hiking, skiing and berry-picking are also permitted. All other activities are prohibited.

Margaree Island National Wildlife Area, Nova Scotia

Margaree Island National Wildlife Area is located in the Gulf of St. Lawrence four kilometres off the coast of Cape Breton, Nova Scotia. The cliffs on the northwest side of the island rise sharply to a height of about fifty metres whereas the southeast side slopes more gradually toward the water. The vegetation of this small exposed island consists of dense white spruce stands on the lee

Margaree Island National Wildlife Area

side and a shrub-grass cover with stunted white spruce on the windward side.

Margaree Island National Wildlife Area is the site of breeding colonies of great blue heron, great cormorant, common tern, black guillemot, herring gull and great black-backed gull. Wildlife observation, hiking and berry-picking are the only activities permitted.

Boot Island National Wildlife Area, Nova Scotia

Boot Island National Wildlife Area is located in the Minas Basin near the mouth of the Gaspereau River, eight kilometres northeast of Wolfville, Kings County, Nova Scotia. It consists of a small upland section, which is about six metres above mean high tide, and an adjoining expanse of salt marsh.

The upland is vegetated with a stand of dense white spruce and a shrub-grass cover. Boot Island National Wildlife Area is an important staging and migration area for waterfowl and to a lesser extent a migration site for shorebirds. It hosts breeding colonies of herring gull, great black-backed gull, great blue heron and double-crested cormorant, and is the site of a large winter crow-roost. Hunting is permitted subject to provincial and federal regulations. Wildlife observation and the picking of greens and wild berries are also permitted.

Sand Pond National Wildlife Area, Nova Scotia

Sand Pond National Wildlife Area lies just two kilometres inland from the tidal waters of the Argyle River on the southwestern coast of Nova Scotia, thirty-two kilometres east of Yarmouth. The area is comprised of two shallow freshwater wetlands, a bog and an expanse of forest and heath covered uplands. The shallow rocky soil, which is typical of southwestern Nova Scotia, is responsible for the lack of tree cover on much of the uplands.

Sand Pond National Wildlife Area provides staging, migration and a limited amount of production habitat for waterfowl. The uplands afford nesting and migration habitat for woodcock and several songbird species such as sparrows, warblers and finches.

Fishing, hunting and trapping are permitted subject to provincial and federal regulations. Wildlife observation, canoeing, hiking, skiing and berry-picking are also permitted.

Port Joli and Port Hebert National Wildlife Areas, Nova Scotia

Located twenty-four kilometres southwest of Liverpool, Queens County, Nova Scotia, these two areas consist of the upper portions of two adjacent coastal inlets and bordering forested areas. The outstanding features of the sheltered inlets of Port Joli and Port Hebert are extensive mud and sand flats which are vegetated largely by beds of eelgrass. The flats are bordered by salt marsh, sand and gravel bars, and boulder-strewn shores. The adjoining woodlands are composed mainly of red maple, red oak, birch, spruce, balsam fir and white pine.

The coastal area, including Port Joli and Port Hebert Inlets, hosts a large overwintering population of Canada geese and a substantial number of black ducks and several sea duck species. Several thousand waterfowl frequent the area for varying lengths of time during the fall migration period. The inlets also afford habitat for a small number of shorebirds and marine birds, and the adjoining woodlands are populated by several species of land birds and mammals.

Waterfowl hunting and wildlife observation are the principal activities undertaken on the area, although major sections of the two inlets are also migratory bird sanctuaries and within their limits hunting is prohibited.

Sand Pond National Wildlife Area

TABLE 4   NATIONAL WILDLIFE AREAS

MAP REF.	NAME	GRID/LOCATION	YEAR EST.	SIZE (ha)	ECOSYSTEM	MAJOR SPECIES
16	Portage Island	E4 Northeast New Brunswick	1979	439.0	saltmarsh, dune communities	migrating waterfowl, shorebirds, osprey, great blue heron
17	Portobello Creek	C3 Saint John River, Southeast New Brunswick	1981	1,780.3	floodplain marsh, forest	waterfowl, songbirds, ungulates
18	Shepody	C5 Southeast New Brunswick	1980	978.6	fresh/salt marsh	waterfowl, shorebirds
19	Tintamarre	C5 Southeast New Brunswick	1978	1,990.0	wetlands, forest	marsh birds, muskrat, marsh hawk, waterfowl
20	Cape Jourimain	D6 Gulf of St. Lawrence New Brunswick	1980	589.0	saltmarsh, beach/dunes	migrating waterfowl, shorebirds
21	Chignecto	C5 Northern Nova Scotia	1980	1,020.0	saltmarsh, upland	Canada geese, ducks
22	Wallace Bay	C6 Northumberland Shore Nova Scotia	1980	585.0	marine/freshwater wetland, forested upland	Canada geese, ducks, muskrat, bald eagle
23	Sand Pond	A4 Yarmouth County, Nova Scotia	1978	521.4	wetlands, forest, heath	migrating waterfowl, songbirds
24	Margaree Island	D8 Cape Breton Nova Scotia	NP	54.0	white spruce, shrub-grass	great blue heron, cormorant, common tern, black guillemot
25	Boot Island	C5 Minas Basin Nova Scotia	1979	144.0	saltmarsh, upland	migrating waterfowl, great blue heron, doublecrested cormorant
26	Port Joli	A5 Southwest Shore Nova Scotia	NP	50.1	saltmarsh, woodland	Canada geese, black duck, sea ducks
27	Port Hebert	A5 Southwest Shore Nova Scotia	NP	41.9	saltmarsh, woodland	Canada geese, black duck, sea ducks
	TOTAL (12)			8,193.3		

NP — Not Proclaimed (areas have been only recently acquired)

Federal Migratory Bird Sanctuaries

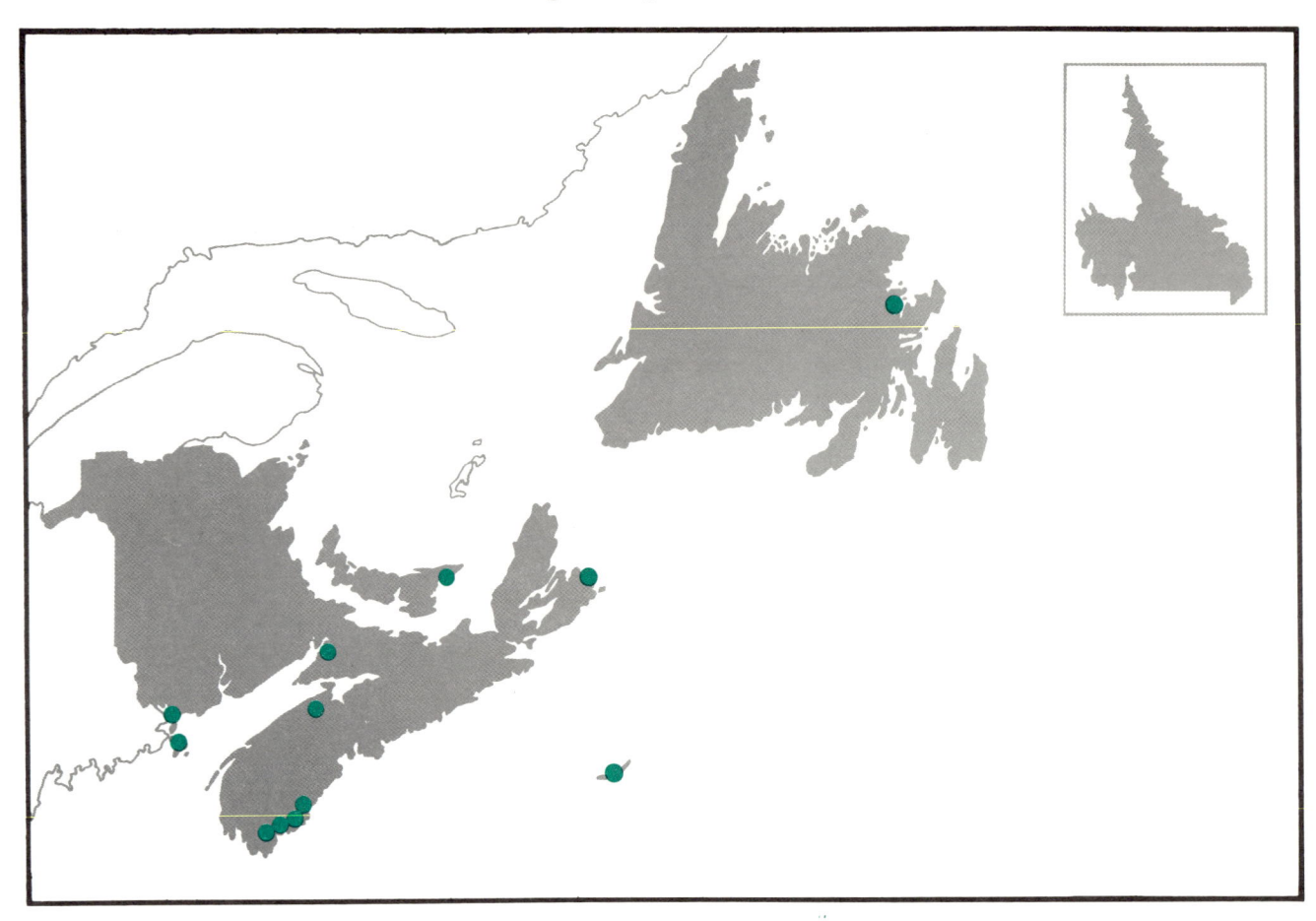

Federal migratory bird sanctuaries are administered by the Canadian Wildlife Service on behalf of the federal government. They are created pursuant to the Migratory Birds Convention Act which became one of the earliest pieces of conservation legislation in Canada when it was passed in 1917. At that time, the United States passed similar legislation to afford protection to the international resource which migratory birds represent.

There are twelve federal migratory bird sanctuaries in the Atlantic Region. Eight are located in Nova Scotia, two are located in New Brunswick, and one each in Prince Edward Island and Newfoundland.

In contrast to most national wildlife areas, hunting is not permitted under any circumstances and people must not carry on any activity that is harmful to migratory birds, their eggs, nests or habitat.

Grand Manan Migratory Bird Sanctuary, New Brunswick

The Sanctuary is situated on the southeast coast of Grand Manan Island, Charlotte County, between the communities of Grand Harbour and Seal Cove. Established in 1931, it adjoins "The Anchorage", a provincial park and campground.

Two large ponds (Long and Great Pond) dominate this 100-hectare sanctuary. The ponds are separated from the sea by a wide sand and gravel barrier beach backed by dunes which are thickly vegetated with beach grass. Surrounding the ponds to the west is a low shrubby bog-heath gradually changing to low spruce-fir forest. Little aquatic growth occurs within the ponds, however a small section of grass-dominated marshland occurs at the outlet of Great Pond.

According to old warden reports several thousand waterfowl used to be observed in the sanctuary. However, numbers have now diminished to a few hundred. During fall migration black ducks, goldeneye and a few geese can usually be found on the ponds along with a small number of ring-necked ducks, pintail and wigeon. During spring, large numbers of eider ducks and brant geese use the area along the beach.

Machias Seal Island Migratory Bird Sanctuary, New Brunswick

Machias Seal Island is located twenty kilometres off the southwestern tip of Grand Manan Island in the Bay of Fundy. It is a small, sparsely vegetated island only about one thousand metres long, by four hundred metres wide. It once was a serious shipping hazard to man until a permanent lighthouse was built in 1832. The lighthouse is still in operation today. A lush green meadow covers the higher parts of the island and provides a striking contrast to the rocky, wave-battered shores.

The most numerous and obvious bird is the arctic tern with approximately 1400 nesting pairs, but their numbers have been decreasing. Approximately 2100 pairs nested here in 1974, and the numbers may have been as high as five thousand pairs during the 1940's. Approximately one hundred pairs of common terns also nest on Machias Seal Island. This is home to one of the most southerly colonies of the common puffin (nine hundred pairs) whose breeding range extends north all the way to Greenland. The other member of the Auk family that nests on Machias Seal Island is the razorbill. It is larger than the puffin with immaculate black and white plumage and a distinctive white ring around the bill.
Approximately one hundred pairs nest here. Though rarely seen by the visitor because it forages at sea or hides in its nesting burrows, the Leach's Storm petrel also breeds here. Fifty-seven active burrows were recorded in 1982.

Besides the seabirds, a few land birds, including the savannah sparrow, spotted sandpiper, tree swallow and barn swallow nest on Machias Seal Island. The list of migrants and incidental visitors is extremely impressive (to date well over one hundred) including several uncommon and rare species. Annually, over 1200 naturalists and photographers visit the sanctuary.

Amherst Point Migratory Bird Sanctuary, Nova Scotia

Five kilometres southwest of Amherst, at the Head of the Bay of Fundy, lies the Amherst Point Migratory Bird Sanctuary. It was established in 1947 with the agreement of the landowners. However, to afford permanent habitat protection the land was later acquired by the Canadian Wildlife Service (1973/74) and designated as a component of the Chignecto National Wildlife Area.

Puffin, Machias Seal Island Migratory Bird Sanctuary

The landscape is a mosaic of ponds, marshes, forests, and old farm fields. Past geological events are responsible for the conical depressions called "sinkholes" that occur in the gypsum deposits which underly the area.

Most of the more than two hundred species of birds that have been observed at Amherst Point Migratory Bird Sanctuary are found there regularly. The diversity and richness of its habitats and the strategic location of the sanctuary on a much-used migration route account for its unusual attractiveness and importance to birds. Waterfowl and other marshbirds are particularly abundant and include most species commonly found in the Atlantic provinces. Black duck, pintail, green-winged teal, blue-winged teal, American wigeon, northern shoveler, ring-necked duck, pie-billed grebe, American bittern and sora nest in the sanctuary. Scaup, common goldeneye, scoters and mergansers are regular migrants. However, the sanctuary's wildlife values are most strikingly exemplified by the occurrence of various unusual waterfowl and marshbirds. Gadwall, redhead, ruddy duck, virginia rail, common gallinule, American coot and black tern have all nested there regularly in the past few years. Stray European waterfowl and several southern waders have also appeared. Many of these species have also been reported at other locations in the Atlantic provinces, however, the sanctuary hosts an unusually large number of species of limited occurrence and distribution in the region.

Haley Lake Migratory Bird Sanctuary, Nova Scotia

Established in 1980, Haley Lake is located in Shelburne County, approximately midway between Port Hebert Harbour and Sable River Estuary.

Typical of most lakes of the granite-based southern uplands of Nova Scotia, Haley Lake is shallow and rocky. Several prominent rock outcroppings surrounded by gravel bars lie within the one hundred hectare lake. Its waters and substrate of low nutrient content are incapable of supporting more than scattered plant life. Its shores of large granite boulders are encroached upon by thick shrub growths of sweet gale and speckled alder, and to the east and west of the lake the land rises abruptly and encloses the lake with prominent woodland ridges. During the early fall period, Canada geese and black duck fly into Haley Lake from the surrounding salt water harbours and estuaries. The principal flight times into the lake are during rising tides when feeding sites in the harbour become inundated. Waterfowl spend most of their time preening and resting on the rock ledges in the lake and on the granite boulders along the shores. The lake also affords the waterfowl fresh water and gravel. Haley Lake has for a number of years been one of the principal fresh water lakes in the area to be frequented by fall flights of geese and black ducks. Records indicate that the number present at any one time does not normally exceed one thousand, however it is probable that many more occur over a period of time.

A small colony of great blue herons nest on two of the rocky ledges within the lake. The colony has been in existence at least since 1944 and is the only known instance of ground nesting herons in the Maritimes.

Port Joli and Port Hebert Migratory Bird Sanctuaries, Nova Scotia

While physically separate sanctuaries, Port Joli and Port Hebert were created to protect similar features. They are located less than two kilometres apart at the heads of two of the most prominent coastal inlets of the region, about midway between the towns of Liverpool and Shelburne on Nova Scotia's southwestern shore. Both sanctuaries have recently been adjoined by national wildlife areas.

The upper reaches of the inlets are some ten kilometres from the outer coastline. The landscape is characterized by low hills and smooth-topped ridges with intervening lakes and bogs and a ragged line of low areas and prominent inlets along the coast. Large mud flats support luxuriant growths of eelgrass, the plant which is largely responsible for the area's importance as migration and winter habitat for waterfowl. Associated with the mudflat flora is an abundance of marine invertebrates.

The Canada goose is the principal waterfowl species, with flocks sometimes in excess of five thousand birds occurring throughout the migration season. Three to five thousand of these geese overwinter in the area.

The inlets afford food and shelter for several other waterfowl species. Second in abundance to Canada geese are black ducks, with up to three thousand often being present. Green-winged teal and northern pintail frequent the inlets briefly during late summer and early fall before moving farther south. Diving ducks including common goldeneye, bufflehead, scaup, scoter and merganser arrive in the area later than the other waterfowl and remain for the winter.

Port Hebert Migratory Bird Sanctuary

Big Glace Bay Lake Migratory Bird Sanctuary, Nova Scotia

The site, established in 1939 lies just east of the town of Glace Bay, Cape Breton County.

Big Glace Bay "Lake" is actually a barrier-beach pond adjacent to the open Atlantic Ocean, and thus subject to daily tidal fluctuations. The 240-hectare site is protected from the open sea by a 1.5 kilometre sand and gravel beach backed by salt marsh and intertidal flats. The shallow brackish-saline water supports beds of eelgrass and thus is attractive to migrating waterfowl. The upland on the east side of the "Lake" is vegetated with stunted spruce while the surrounding upland on the western side is incorporated into the town of Glace Bay and support a heavy water plant and thermal power generating facility.

At least two pairs of piping plovers nest on the Glace Bay barrier beach and several pairs of common terns nest on the salt marsh hummocks behind the beach. The principal use by waterfowl is during fall and winter when over one hundred black ducks and several hundred geese use the area along with forty to sixty common goldeneye and a few bufflehead.

Kentville Migratory Bird Sanctuary, Nova Scotia

The sanctuary, which dates from 1939, lies just west of the town of Kentville, Kings County, a portion of the area being within the town boundaries.

This 200-hectare wetland is a flood plain marsh with numerous small shallow ponds and backwaters along the meandering course of the Cornwallis River. The river varies in depth from one to three metres and is slightly brackish at the eastern end of the sanctuary where there is a slight tidal influence.

The wetland is dominated by reed-canary grass. Bluejoint, spike rush, and a wide variety of pondweeds and other aquatic plants occur within this fertile wetland.

A few broods of black ducks and blue-winged teal are annually produced on the area. During late summer and throughout the fall, flocks of mixed waterfowl species numbering between eighty and two hundred usually occur within the sanctuary.

Sable River Migratory Bird Sanctuary, Nova Scotia

This sanctuary is located on the Sable River estuary one kilometre south of Highway 103 at the community of Sable River in Shelburne County. It has been part of the community since 1941.

This 260-hectare sanctuary includes the inner portion of the Sable River estuary, including all shoals, rocks and islets up to the mean high tide mark on the adjoining upland. Scattered small salt marshes occur along both the east and west sides and eelgrass dominates the shallow nearshore waters out to the much deeper mid-channel. The mid-channel area remains ice-free in all but the severest of winters, a feature that makes the site particularly attractive to the overwintering Canada goose population.

The sanctuary is used throughout the fall by several hundred Canada geese and black ducks along with smaller numbers of green-winged teal and a variety of other waterfowl. However, during severe winters most of the habitat at the nearby Port Joli and Port Hebert sanctuaries freezes over for a short period during mid to late January. At that time the overwintering Canada goose population in the area moves to the Sable River section which remains ice-free in the mid channel.

Sable Island Migratory Bird Sanctuary, Nova Scotia

Sable Island is situated approximately 180 kilometres southeast of Canso, Nova Scotia, and three hundred kilometres east of Halifax, in the Atlantic Ocean. The sanctuary was set aside in 1977.

It is composed of a crescent of sand extending along an east-west axis for approximately thirty-two kilometres. The island consists of twenty kilometres of consolidated dunes and long unstabilized terminal bars at each end.

Its maximum width is 1.5 kilometres and the highest dunes approach thirty metres. The north beach is steep and narrow, whereas the south beach is wide and flat. Beach grass dominates and stabilizes the dunes. Between the dunes are numerous depressions usually filled with freshwater and supporting a variety of aquatic plants. These small ponds are most numerous near the west end.

A ten-kilometre-long salt water lake is located on the south beach about mid-way along the island.

Sable Island is the only known nesting place for the Ipswich sparrow, a subspecies of the savannah sparrow. Over 2,500 pairs of terns (about 60% arctic) nest on the island along with over five hundred pairs of black-backed gulls and two thousand pairs of herring gulls. A few sandpipers and semipalmated plovers nest on the island and broods of black ducks and red-breasted mergansers are produced near the ponds.

There are approximately three hundred Sable Island ponies living wild on the island. They were introduced by Rev. Andrew LeMercier, a French Huguenot priest from Boston attempting to colonize the island in 1738. Large numbers of harbour and grey seals also breed on Sable Island.

Sable Island Ponies, Sable Island Migratory Bird Sanctuary

Black Pond Migratory Bird Sanctuary, Prince Edward Island

Black Pond is situated along Highway #16, five kilometres east of the town of Souris, Prince Edward Island.

This 130-hectare site is an exceptional example of a barrier-beach pond ecosystem. A one-kilometre-wide sand beach separates the fifty-hectare pond from the sea. Black Pond itself is a shallow freshwater lake filled with dense beds of pondweed and bordered by spike rushes and scattered stands of cattail and bullrushes. The surrounding countryside is lowland with small white spruce woodlots and agricultural fields.

This vegetation complex provides the most important waterfowl production and migration habitat in eastern Prince Edward Island. Nesting waterfowl species include black ducks, green-winged teal, blue-winged teal, ring-necked ducks, and occasionally, common goldeneye.

During migration the sanctuary is a major waterfowl concentration area, with flocks of ducks numbering from several hundred to about one thousand individuals. Large flocks of blue-winged teal and lesser numbers of pintail and American wigeon use the sanctuary in September, generally leaving by early October. Flocks of green-winged teal and ring-necked ducks stay well into November, while flocks of black ducks numbering from four to six hundred stay until Black Pond freezes over in mid-December. Small flocks of Canada geese and brant are commonly observed in the sanctuary during spring migration.

Terra Nova Migratory Bird Sanctuary, Newfoundland

The sanctuary, set up in 1967, is situated in the Bonavista Bay region of northeastern Newfoundland, adjacent to Terra Nova National Park.

The site consists of the upper portions of two tidal inlets that are nearly totally enclosed by lands within Terra Nova National Park. The northern portion consists of Broad Cove and Southwest Arm, which are separated by a causeway and bridge. The other section is comprised of the most westerly portion of Newman Sound. The areas are relatively shallow tidal inlets with intertidal flats in their upper reaches, the largest one being Big Brook tidal flats at the head of Newman Sound.

The areas are not extensively used by migratory birds, however, a few hundred Canada geese, black ducks, goldeneye and mergansers use the site during fall migration. The sanctuary was requested by Parks Canada since the park boundaries only extended to the mean high tide mark. It was therefore necessary to close these marine areas to hunting in order to preserve and protect the wildlife in their natural surroundings.

Canada Geese

TABLE 5   FEDERAL MIGRATORY BIRD SANCTUARIES

MAP REF.	NAME	GRID	/LOCATION	YEAR EST.	SIZE (ha)	ECOSYSTEM	MAJOR SPECIES
28	Grand Manan	B3	Grand Manan Island, New Brunswick	1931	250	ponds, beach, dunes	migrating waterfowl, eider, brant
29	Machias Seal Island	B2	Bay of Fundy New Brunswick	1944	10	heath meadow, rocky shore	arctic tern, common puffin, razor-bill, common tern, leach's storm petrel
30	Big Glace Bay Lake	D10	Glace Bay, Nova Scotia	1939	240	barrier beach pond	waterfowl, piping plover, common tern
31	Kentville	C5	Kentville, Nova Scotia	1939	200	floodplain, tussock marsh	black duck, blue-winged teal, migrating waterfowl
32	Port Joli	A5	Southwest Nova Scotia	1941	280	mudflats, saltmarsh	Canada geese, black duck, other waterfowl
33	Port Hebert	A5	Southwest Nova Scotia	1941	350	mudflats, saltmarsh	Canada geese, black duck, other waterfowl
34	Haley Lake	A5	Southwest Nova Scotia	1980	100	freshwater lake, woodland	Canada geese, black duck, great blue heron
35	Sable River	A4	Southwest Nova Scotia	1941	260	estuary, saltmarsh	Canada geese, black duck
36	Amherst Point	C5	Amherst, Nova Scotia	1947	433	wetlands, forest, fields	waterfowl, marshbirds
37	Sable Island	A10	Atlantic Ocean, off Nova Scotia	1977	2,350	beaches, dunes	Ipswich sparrow, arctic and common tern, Sable ponies, shorebirds, seals
38	Black Pond	D7	Souris, Prince Edward Island	1936	130	barrier beach pond	waterfowl, Canada geese, black duck
39	Terra Nova	F16	Northeast Newfoundland	1967	870	tidal inlets, flats	migrating waterfowl, Canada geese, black duck, shore birds, seabirds
	TOTAL (12)				5,473		

Provincial Parks
NEW BRUNSWICK

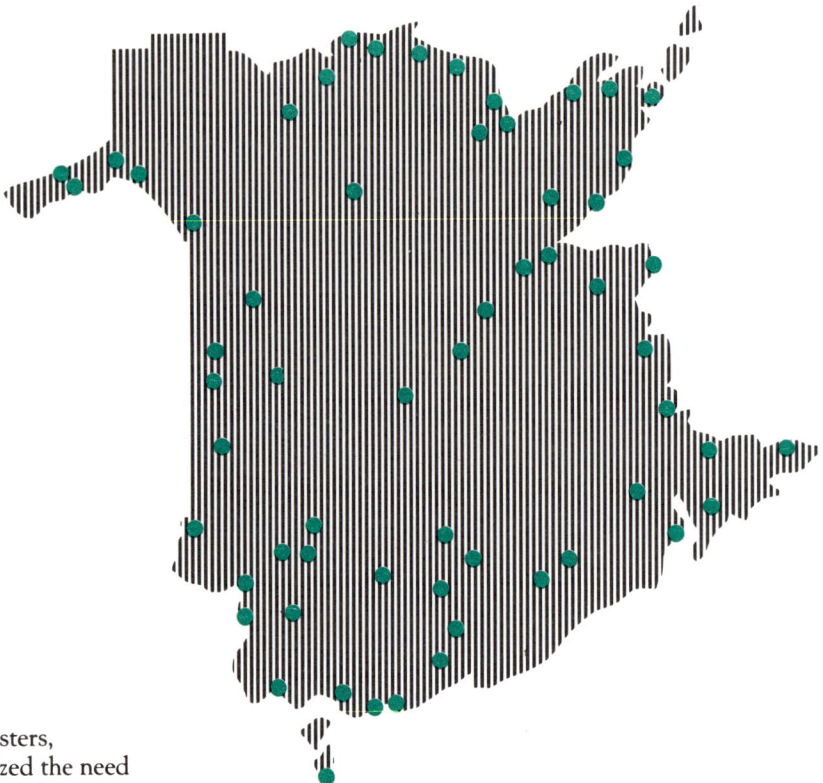

In the 1930's New Brunswick district foresters, independently around the province, recognized the need for automobile travellers in their Model T's and Model A's to stop and rest along their journey's way. They were also concerned with the fire hazard that these same people were causing during their "hot-lunch" breaks. It was from this same impetus that the first provincial park was created in 1935 at Glenwood, located forty kilometres west of Campbellton on Highway 17. Utilizing the better springs and sites, a series of small roadside picnic grounds were established. Primitive by today's standards, these park areas were nevertheless, the humble beginnings of the current province-wide park system.

During the 1950's highway engineers took over the responsibility of fitting roadside rest areas and scenic lookouts into their construction programs. The tourist influx into New Brunswick was increasing at a steady rate, and efforts to cope with the demand could not keep pace. This gave rise to the passage of the Provincial Parks Act in 1961, and in 1963 a separate Parks Branch was formed.

Under the auspices of Tourism New Brunswick since 1970, the province has established a network of 61 parks divided into seven classes, each of which defines the main focus of the park. In several cases, classifications may overlap. For example, a park that has been designated a campground or recreation park, may also have a beach. A listing under one classification designates its primary purpose but does not preclude facilities included in another category. Some provincial parks are under concession to private operators, however, the standards of provincially operated parks are maintained.

Rest Areas

Rest area parks are designated to meet the needs of the travelling public. For the most part, they include picnic facilities and are situated along the province's road system. Generally small, (one to twenty-five hectares) they provide parking, tables, potable water and toilet facilities. They are not intended to provide overnight camping. Picnic grounds may be located to provide viewing sites of natural scenic attractions.

TABLE 6		REST AREA PARKS — NEW BRUNSWICK		
MAP REF.	NAME	GRID/ LOCATION	YEAR OPENED	SIZE (Hectares)
40	Beech Hill	C5	1965	29.07
41	Beechwood	D2	1971	7.89
42	Brockway	C2	Proposed	2.02
43	Castalia	B3	1960	8.09
44	Doaktown	D3	1954	.46
45	Eagle Rock	C3	1959	1.25
46	Glenwood	E2	1935	22.50
47	Greystone	E4	1961	6.76
48	Hartland	D2	1980	2.43
49	Lepreau Falls	C3	1956	8.90
50	Lindsay Spring	D2	1971	.17
51	Lower Kent	D5	1959	1.53
52	Morrisey Rock	E3	1952	.17
53	Pennfield	C3	1957	.66
54	Penobsquis	C4	1954	.28
55	Pine Grove	C4	1963	3.40
56	Pokeshaw	E4	1982	1.96
57	Queenstown	C3	1957	.48
58	St. Croix River	C2	1978	1.94
59	St. Margarets (Bay du Vin River)	D4	under constr.	24.30
60	Tetagouche Falls	E4	1968	20.96
61	Upper Blackville	D4	1951	4.01
62	St. Basile	E1	1955	5.60
	TOTAL (23)			154.83

Campground Parks

Campground parks are designed to meet the needs of resident and non-resident campers for overnight camping. They vary in size up to three hundred organized sites and include parking, tables, potable water and toilets. Supervision is provided and a camping area permit is required. A maximum stay of fourteen days is allowed during the period of June 15th to September 15th.

TABLE 7		CAMPGROUND PARKS — NEW BRUNSWICK		
MAP REF.	NAME	GRID/LOCATION	YEAR OPENED	SIZE (Hectares)
63	Caraquet	E5	1964	3.29
64	Kedgwick	E2	1961	18.82
65	Muniac	D2	1956	2.70
66	Red Pines	D3	1965	21.53
67	St. Leonard	E2	1960	34.30
68	Steeves Mountain	D5	1958	5.70
	TOTAL (6)			86.34

Windsurfers, Mactaquac Provincial Park

Parlee Beach Provincial Park

Beach Parks

Beach Parks are created to meet the need for suitable bathing and swimming areas. They are usually developed in conjunction with picnic grounds, but the prime functions are bathing and swimming. Beach parks provide change houses, tables, potable water and toilets.

TABLE 8		BEACH PARKS — NEW BRUNSWICK		
MAP REF.	NAME	GRID/ LOCATION	YEAR OPENED	SIZE (Hectares)
69	Beresford	E4	1965	4.21
70	Escuminac Beach	E5	1965	9.14
71	Lac Baker	E1	1959	4.59
72	Middle Island	E4	1968	6.88
73	Neguac	E4	1970	58.04
74	Youghall Beach	E4	1970	12.14
75	Parlee Beach	D5	1957	65.84
	TOTAL (7)			160.84

Recreation Parks

Recreation parks are designed to provide a full range of activities, including picnic grounds, campgrounds and beaches, in one park. The larger parks may include both summer and winter recreational activities.

TABLE 9	RECREATION PARKS — NEW BRUNSWICK			
MAP REF.	NAME	GRID/LOCATION	YEAR OPENED	SIZE (Hectares)
76	Anchorage (The)	B3	1970	181.18
77	Chaleur	E3	1967	154.68
78	Enclosure (The)	D4	1951	43.34
79	Frontiére	E1	1971	48.56
80	Grand Lake	C3	1959	85.80
81	Herring Cove	B3	1959	423.80
82	Jacquet River	E3	1956	1.84
83	Jardine	D5	1957	6.88
84	Lake George	C2	1958	45.02
85	Lakeside	C3	1963	47.17
86	Les Jardins de la République	E1	1974	43.52
87	Mactaquac	C3	1965	527.32
88	Murray Beach	D6	1959	26.83
89	New River Beach	C3	1959	337.96
90	North Lake	C2	1968	46.54
91	Oak Bay	C2	1955	13.44
92	Oak Point	C3	1959	21.65
93	Shippagan	E5	1961	49.51
94	Spednic Lake	C2		346.73
95	Sunbury-Oromocto	C3	1967	96.13
96	Sugarloaf	E3	1971	1,142.05
97	Rocks (The)	C5	1958	15.04
98	Val Comeau	E5	1963	22.07
	TOTAL (23)			3,727.06

Moose

Wildlife Parks

Wildlife parks are established primarily to provide a public display of animals and birds native to the Province of New Brunswick. They may be developed in conjunction with picnic grounds, campgrounds or beaches. Currently, there is only one provincially owned wildlife park in the province at Woolastook, which is privately operated under contract.

TABLE 10		WILDLIFE PARKS — NEW BRUNSWICK		
MAP REF.	NAME	GRID/LOCATION	YEAR OPENED	SIZE (Hectares)
99	Woolastook	C3	1968	509.67

Resource Parks

Mount Carleton is currently the only resource park in the provincial system. A large, multiple-use park area, it's primary function is to provide a large block of land for the enjoyment of outdoor recreation in a natural environment. However, only a small portion of the total area is developed formally. Fishing is allowed on a controlled basis, while hunting and trapping are not allowed. The harvesting of natural resources is allowed under controlled supervision and is intended to demonstrate the sustainable use of renewable resources. Mount Carleton is also designated as a provincial wildlife management area.

TABLE 11		RESOURCE PARKS — NEW BRUNSWICK		
MAP REF.	NAME	GRID/LOCATION	YEAR OPENED	SIZE (Hectares)
100	Mount Carleton	E2	1970	17,427.19

Marine Parks

At present, a feasibility study is underway to consider establishment of Fundy Isles Marine Park which, if created, would become the first marine provincial park in New Brunswick. Marine parks are intended to be areas that will be reached primarily by boat and will have no road access. They will be designed to preserve the natural environment of marine and shore fauna and flora. Primitive facilities will be provided and potable water may not be available.

New Brunswick has also set aside twenty-four areas as park reserves. These areas have no legal status or management regime, but are used as candidates for expansion of the formal provincial park system.

Provincial Parks
NOVA SCOTIA

Nova Scotia's provincial parks system had its beginnings during the 1950's when the Department of Highways established more than one hundred roadside rest areas. The growing demand for outdoor recreation facilities during this period led to the formal establishment of a parks program. The Provincial Parks Act was enacted in 1959, giving the Department of Lands and Forests administrative responsibility for the existing rest areas, and for developing the parks system to meet the objectives of recreation for the public and conservation and preservation of natural areas.

Early parks policy, which called for at least one major camping park in each county, picnic parks at thirty to sixty kilometre intervals on major highways and acquisition of beaches, has largely been achieved. Recent emphasis has been on developing major beach parks such as Risser's and Clam Harbour as well as larger resource-based parks such as Blomidon and Taylor's head. Hiking, canoeing and nature interpretation are part of these new goals.

The existing provincial park system includes 247 sites, of which 108 are operational and 139 are non-operational (park reserves). The Provincial Parks Act is the strongest legislation currently used for establishing protected areas in Nova Scotia, although the recently proclaimed Special Places Act should also prove important. In addition, the Beaches Protection Act and the Lands and Forests Act may be used to protect provincial heritage resources.

The 108 operational parks are divided into the following general classes for statistical purposes: camping, picnic, beach, wildlife, and historic. Although not adopted officially at the policy level, a second, more elaborate classification system comprised of ten classes is used for planning purposes.

Camping Parks

Camping parks are set aside to provide overnight camping facilities for both residents and the travelling public. There are nineteen camping parks in Nova Scotia, many of which also provide picnic and/or beach areas.

Blomidon Provincial Park

TABLE 12 — CAMPING PARKS — NOVA SCOTIA

MAP REF.	NAME	GRID/LOCATION	YEAR OPENED	SIZE (ha)	ASSOCIATED FACILITIES
101	Beaver Mountain	C7	1972	133.0	picnic
102	Caribou	C7	1958	31.6	picnic, beach
103	Salt Springs	C7	1959	31.3	picnic
104	Boylston	C8	1968	90.9	picnic
105	Salsman	C8	1976	10.5	picnic
106	Wentworth	C6	1961	143.0	picnic
107	Five Islands	C5	1966	412.8	picnic
108	Porters Lake	B6	1968	87.4	picnic
109	Laurie	B6	1961	26.3	picnic
110	Smiley's	B6	1960	40.5	picnic
111	Blomidon	C5	1973	695.3	picnic, beach
112	Valleyview	B4	1969	54.2	picnic
113	Graves Island	B5	1971	49.8	picnic
114	Risser's Beach	B5	1973	75.8	picnic, beach
115	Ellenwood Lake	A4	1969	133.7	picnic, beach
116	The Islands	A4	1958	106.0	picnic, beach
117	Whycocomagh	C8	1959	205.2	picnic
118	Mira River	C10	1967	87.3	picnic, beach
119	Battery	C9	1967	45.9	picnic
	TOTAL (19)			2,460.5	

Picnic and Beach Parks

There are seventy-nine picnic and beach parks, set aside to provide rest areas for the motoring public or weekend recreationalists seeking a sunny spot to bathe or relax. Many, but not all of the beach parks have picnic facilities.

TABLE 13 — PICNIC AND BEACH PARKS — NOVA SCOTIA

MAP REF.	NAME	GRID/LOCATION	YEAR PROCLAIMED	SIZE (ha)	CLASS
120	Arisaig	C7	1981	24.7	picnic
121	Greenhill	C7	1975	6.4	picnic
122	Powell's Point	C7	1974	27.1	picnic
123	Melmerby Beach	C7	1974	101.2	beach
124	Rushton Beach	C6	1978	25.5	beach
125	Waterside Beach	C7	1980	80.9	beach
126	Sherbrooke	C8		0.8	picnic
127	Two Mile Lake	C7	1975	3.6	picnic
128	Marie Joseph	B7		0.6	picnic
129	Judd's Pool	B7	1983	80.1	picnic
130	Tatamagouche	C6	1974	5.7	picnic
131	McElmond's Pond	C6		5.7	picnic
132	Gulf Shore	C6	1972	9.3	picnic/beach
133	Shinimacas	C6	1973	7.7	picnic
134	Fenwick	C5		20.2	picnic
135	Northport Beach	C6	1974	10.5	picnic/beach
136	Heather Beach	C6	1980	7.2	beach
137	Tidnish Dock	C5	1982	10.5	picnic
138	Newville Lake	C5	LF	0.2	picnic
139	Musquodoboit Valley	C6	1973	30.4	picnic
140	Spry Bay	B7		0.4	picnic
141	Martinique Beach	B6	1971	60.6	picnic/beach
142	Clam Harbour	B7	1980	393.6	picnic/beach
143	Taylor Head	B7	1980	814.5	picnic/beach
144	Oakfield	B6	1973	53.8	picnic
145	Lewis Lake	B6	1976	149.7	picnic

146	Crystal Crescent Beach	B6	1981	182.9	picnic/beach
147	Queensland Beach	B5	1980	1.3	beach
148	Cleveland Beach	B6	1978	4.3	beach
149	Anthony	C6	1974	7.4	picnic/beach
150	Mt. Uniacke	B6		2.0	picnic
151	Falls Lake	B5	1984	4.9	picnic
152	Coldbrook	C5	1980	3.7	picnic
153	Clairmont	C5	1972	22.7	picnic
154	Lumsden Pond	B5	1981	7.6	picnic/beach
155	Lake George	B5		4.6	beach

Crystal Crescent Beach Provincial Park

PICNIC AND BEACH PARKS — NOVA SCOTIA (Cont'd)

MAP REF.	NAME	GRID/ LOCATION	YEAR PROCLAIMED	SIZE (ha)	CLASS
156	Cottage Cove	C4		0.2	picnic
157	Upper Clements	B4		12.5	picnic
158	Bayswater Beach	B5	1976	4.7	beach
159	East River	B5	1979	0.4	picnic
160	Sim's Settlement	B5		4.0	picnic
161	Maitland	B5		0.5	picnic
162	Second Peninsula	B5	1975	18.6	picnic
163	Card Lake	B5	1976	113.3	picnic
164	Ninevah	B5		8.1	picnic
165	Fancy Lake	B5		0.2	picnic
166	Ten Mile Lake	B5	1975	3.2	picnic
167	Cameron's Brook	B5	1981	1.2	picnic
168	Summerville Beach	A5		22.7	beach
169	Glenwood	A4	1983	46.7	picnic
170	Port Maitland Beach	A3	1976	6.9	beach
171	Sable River	A4	1982	27.8	picnic
172	Sand Hill Beach	A4	1976	82.2	beach
173	Lake Midway	B3	1981	0.8	picnic
174	Savory	B4	1974	10.8	picnic
175	Smuggler's Cove	B3	1983	3.6	picnic
176	Mavilette Beach	B3	1983	101.2	beach
177	Central Grove	B3	1976	11.7	picnic
178	North River	D9		191.0	picnic
179	Plaster	D9	1973	12.1	picnic
180	Cabot's Landing	D9	1974	6.9	picnic/beach
181	Dalem Lake	D9	1977	73.7	picnic
182	St. Ann's	D9	1983	2.4	picnic
183	Cape Smokey	D9	1983	168.8	picnic
184	MacCormack Park	C9		3.6	picnic
185	Long Point	C8	1973	1.6	picnic
186	Lake-O-Law	D9	1974	2.0	picnic

Martinique Beach Provincial Park

187	Mabou	D8	1974	2.2	picnic
188	S.W. Margaree	D8	1975	7.1	picnic
189	Barachois	D9	1983	118.8	picnic
190	Ben Eoin	C9	1975	90.6	picnic
191	Dominion Beach	D10		23.2	beach
192	Grove's Point	D9	1980	4.7	picnic
193	Lennox Passage	C8		34.0	picnic
194	Arichat	C8		0.04	picnic
195	Kempt Road	C8		0.4	picnic
196	Point Michaud Beach	C9		60.1	beach
197	Pondville Beach	C9	1984	2.8	beach
198	Irish Cove	C9	LF	2.9	picnic
	TOTAL (79)			3,462.54	

LF = Leased from private owner

Wildlife Parks/Historic Parks/Boat Ramps

In addition to camping and picnic/beach parks there are five boat ramps operated by provincial parks, one of which is on (leased) private land. There are also three wildlife parks, one historical park, and the provincial parks division office lands which are included in the 108 operational sites.

The province also has 139 provincial park reserves which have some protection in that they have been withdrawn for future consideration as provincial parks under the Provincial Parks Act. This represents an additional 10,105.58 hectares of land which has interim protection from development. Many of these reserves will ultimately become provincial parks, but some may become redundant as the Province continues evaluating these properties in relationship to changing provincial park program objectives and priorities.

TABLE 14 WILDLIFE PARKS/HISTORIC PARKS/BOAT RAMPS NOVA SCOTIA

MAP REF.	NAME	GRID/ LOCATION	YEAR OPENED	SIZE (ha)	CLASS
199	Barachois Harbour	D9		9.0	boat ramp
200	Hubbards	B5		0.3	boat ramp
201	Bush Island	B5	LF	0.03	boat ramp
202	Dundee	C8		62.83	boat ramp
203	Louisdale	C8		0.14	boat ramp
204	Shubenacadie*	C6	1950	72.8	wildlife park
205	Upper Clements**	B4	1976	303.5	wildlife park
206	Two Rivers	C9	1976	190.2	wildlife park
207	Balmoral Mills	C6		8.4	historic park
208	Parks Office — Debert	C6		4.2	Administration (no park facilities)
	TOTAL (10)			651.4	

LF = Leased from private owner
 * = Proclaimed as a wildlife management area but a portion is operated as a provincial wildlife park.
** = Proclaimed as a game sanctuary, but operated as a provincial wildlife park.

Provincial Parks
PRINCE EDWARD ISLAND

The Prince Edward Island provincial parks system began with the private donation of several properties in the late 1950's. The Provincial Parks Act was passed in 1956 and provided the authority to create provincial parks, principally to provide public areas for the benefit, pleasure and enjoyment of the people of Prince Edward Island. The first provincial park in Prince Edward Island was Strathgartney — officially opened July 1, 1959. More land was acquired (by private donation or government purchase) over the next two decades to provide additional day use and campground parks.

In 1965 the Provincial Parks Act was included under the framework of the Recreation Development Act which had broader powers for land acquisition, beach and natural area protection and park development.

Throughout its history, park administration has been contained in a number of divisions and departments of the provincial government. Since 1980, it has rested with the Department of Transportation and Public Works. The goals of providing public lands for recreation and protection of beaches have largely been achieved. The Parks Branch is now upgrading existing parks as well as working towards the goal of preservation of natural areas and interpretation of natural history phenomena.

The Prince Edward Island provincial park system is currently comprised of thirty-six parks which fall into five different classes.

Nature Preserves are intended to protect and perpetuate in an undisturbed state, individual features of unique natural significance, possessing natural conditions of scientific and/or educational value. This is the most restrictive category of provincial parks and controls are required to protect the integrity of the natural environment. At present, only one area (Townshend Woodlot) is designated a nature preserve. However many other areas have been identified as warranting protection for their natural values and have been acquired. The province is currently considering ways of protecting these areas. (See section on Ecological Reserves — Prince Edward Island)

Natural Environment Parks are natural lands set aside to educate and acquaint the user with the aesthetics and values of the natural landscapes and to provide associated compatible forms of recreation. Only Cable Head and Sir. Andrew MacPhail have been designated as natural environment parks.

Recreation Parks are established to provide areas that are adaptable to heavy use and offer a wide range of outdoor recreation opportunities. The principal activity is usually camping, although day-use facilities are also provided. This category and Wayside/Beach Access Parks are the most common in the provincial system, together comprising thirty-three of the thirty-six park units.

Wayside/Beach Access Parks are created to promote a safe and pleasurable travel experience. They are set aside at reasonable intervals for motorists to stop and rest, or to provide access facilities for good beaches.

Historic Parks are created to preserve, restore, and interpret buildings, sites, objects and related lands of historical, educational and cultural interest. This category is not frequently used in the provincial system, and at present only two parks have historic significance.

TABLE 15 — PROVINCIAL PARKS — PRINCE EDWARD ISLAND

MAP REF.	NAME	GRID/ LOCATION	YEAR ACQUIRED	SIZE (ha)	CLASS
209	Anglo	D6	1962	7.3	recreation
210	Argyle	D6	1961	19.4	beach access
211	Belmont	D6	1966	11.3	wayside
212	Bloomfield	D6	1964	5.3	wayside
213	Bonshaw	D6	1955	2.4	wayside
214	Brookvale	D6	1967	20.2	recreation
215	Brudenell River	D7	1958	563.3	recreation
216	Buffaloland	D7	1970	62.3	wayside
217	Cable Head	D7	1973	427.8	natural environment
218	Cabot	D6	1961	138.4	recreation
219	Campbell's Cove	D7	1963	10.1	recreation
220	Cedar Dunes	D5	1963	57.1	recreation
221	Chelton	D6	1976	7.3	beach access
222	Crowbush Cove	D7	1980	32.4	recreation
223	Fantasyland	D7	1968	8.1	recreation
224	Green	D6	1960	95.1	recreation/historic
225	Jacques Cartier	D5	1960	11.3	recreation
226	Linkletter	D6	1959	29.5	recreation
227	Lord Selkrik	D7	1958	60.3	recreation
228	Marie	D7	1963	2.4	wayside
229	Mill River	D5	1970	183.7	recreation
230	Mt. Stewart	D7	1965	6.1	wayside
231	Northumberland	C7	1967	30.8	recreation
232	Panmure	D7	1967	35.2	recreation
233	Pinette	D7	1959	3.2	beach access
234	Red Point	D7	1961	6.5	recreation
235	Scales Pond	D6	1967	6.5	wayside/historic

236	Sir Andrew MacPhail	D7	1961	56.6	natural environment
237	Souris Beach	D7	1976	15.0	beach access
238	St. Peters	D7	1961	6.9	recreation
239	Strathgartney	D6	1958	28.3	recreation
240	Tea Hill	D6	1978	6.9	beach access
241	Townshend Woodlot	D7	1970	102.0	nature preserve
242	Union Corner	D6	1958	3.2	beach access
243	Victoria	D6	1961	7.3	beach access
244	Wood Islands	C7	1967	12.1	wayside
	TOTAL (36)			2,081.6	

Red Point Provincial Park

Provincial Parks
NEWFOUNDLAND AND LABRADOR

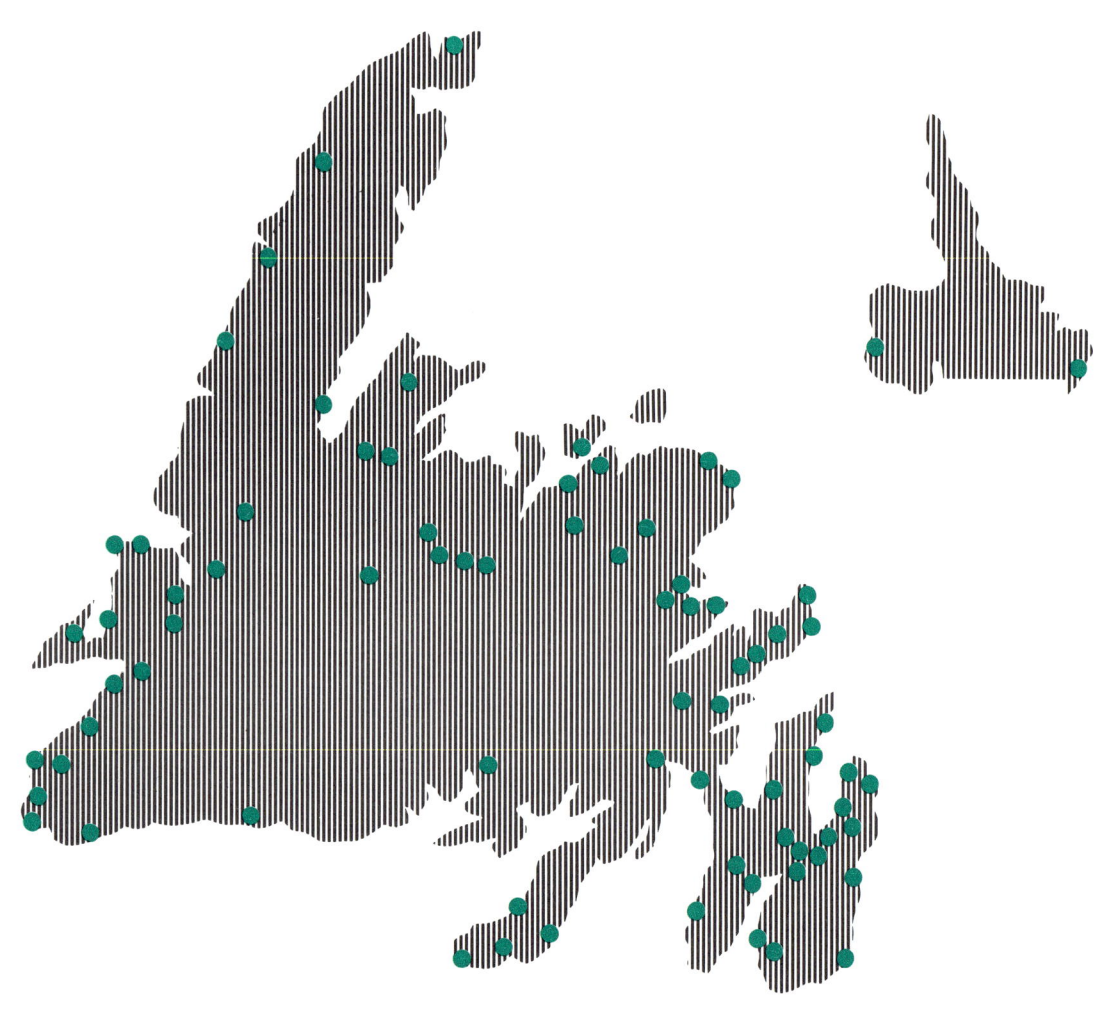

Newfoundland and Labrador celebrated the 30th anniversary of the establishment of its first provincial park in 1984. The Provincial Parks Act was passed in 1952 and in 1954 the first provincial park, Sir Richard Squires Memorial Park, was established at Big Falls on the Humber River.

The provincial park system and its administration has progressed through a number of phases. During the early years the emphasis was on day use and camping parks, particularly in proximity to the Trans-Canada Highway which was completed across the province in 1965.

The focus changed in the early 1970's to the development of beach and swimming areas off the Trans-Canada Highway. During the late 1970's, Natural Scenic Attraction Parks were inaugurated and efforts were made to provide visitor information and education. Hiking trails and major exhibits were constructed and interpretive publications produced.

Most recently an attempt is being made to diversify outdoor experiences by providing winter camping and cross-country skiing facilities and an inventory of canoe routes.

The provincial parks are administered by the Parks Division of the Department of Culture, Recreation and Youth. There are currently seventy-seven provincial parks in Newfoundland and Labrador which are divided into three categories.

Camping Parks

From a total of seventy-seven parks, forty-two offer primitive camping opportunities and one (Grand Codroy) provides both primitive and serviced sites. In all, over 2,200 sites are provided for a variety of camping equipment, from tents to camper-trailers. All sites have picnic tables and fire pits. In addition to camping, most of these parks also have day-use areas which include facilities for picnicking, swimming, boating and angling. Pit toilets and drinking water are provided throughout the camping and picnic grounds. All of these camping parks are staffed during the operation season. The larger parks open on the Victoria Day weekend (May 24th) while the remainder open mid-June. All parks close after the Labour Day weekend, with the exception of those offering organized winter recreation activities.

TABLE 16 CAMPING PARKS — NEWFOUNDLAND AND LABRADOR

MAP REF.	NAME	GRID/ LOCATION	YEAR OPENED	SIZE (ha)
245	Chance Cove	D16	1974	2,068
246	La Manche	E17	1966	1,394
247	Butter Pot	E16	1964	1,752
248	Gushue's Pond	E16	1961	179
249	Holyrood Pond	D16	1973	226
250	Fitzgerald's Pond	E16	1972	813
251	Backside Pond	E16	1972	562
252	Northern Bay Sands	E16	1966	14
253	Bellevue Beach	E16	1959	131
254	Jack's Pond	E16	1959	601
255	Freshwater Pond	E14	1973	892
256	Frenchman's Cove	E14	1967	51
257	Lockston Path	F16	1966	202
258	Piper's Hole River	E15	1976	497
259	Square Pond	F15	1960	39
260	David Smallwood	F15	1966	51
261	Windmill Bight	G16	1966	365
262	Jonathan's Pond	G15	1966	446
263	Notre Dame	G14	1959	113
264	Dildo Run	G15	1967	327
265	Beothuck	F14	1968	74
266	Jipujijkuei Kuespem	E14	1976	882
267	Mary March	F13	1969	32
268	Catamaran	G13	1960	42
269	Indian River	G13	1959	29

270	Baie Verte	G13	1961	14
271	Flatwater Pond	G13	1968	95
272	Squires Memorial	G12	1954	1,574
273	Sop's Arm	G13	1966	10
274	River of Ponds	H12	1966	120
275	Pistolet Bay	114	1974	890
276	Pinware River	X3	1974	68
277	Duley Lake	X1	1973	882
278	Blow Me Down	G11	1972	226
279	Blue Ponds	F11	1961	125
280	Piccadilly Head	F11	1966	42
281	Barachois Pond	F11	1961	3,497
282	Crabbe's River	F11	1959	3
283	Grand Codroy	E10	1966	23
284	Mummichog	E10	1971	84
285	Cheeseman	E10	1960	206
286	Otter Bay	E11	1969	162
287	Sandbanks	E12	1973	230
	TOTAL (43)			20,033

Northern Bay Sands Provincial Park

Day Use Parks

Fifteen parks are designed solely for those wishing to spend an enjoyable day in a natural setting. Facilities usually include picnic sites with tables. Drinking water and pit toilets are available and some of these parks offer recreational pursuits such as swimming, angling and hiking. All day-use parks are open to the public from 8 a.m. to 10 p.m. each day. While most of these parks are not staffed, they are operated by staff from nearby camping parks. Camping is not permitted in day-use parks.

TABLE 17 DAY USE PARKS — NEWFOUNDLAND AND LABRADOR

MAP REF.	NAME	GRID/ LOCATION	YEAR OPENED	SIZE (ha)
288	Cochrane Pond	E17	1960	21
289	Father Duffy's Well	E16	1959	9
290	Thorburn Lake	F15	1972	35
291	Smith Sound	F16	1972	18
292	Soldier's Pond	E17	1975	7
293	South West Pond	E16	1975	4
294	Marine Drive	E17	1981	783
295	Glenwood	F15	1962	92
296	Dog Bay Pond	G15	1972	4
297	Aspen Brook	F14	1960	40
298	Pearson's Peak	F14	1966	N/A
299	Three Mile Lake	H13	1972	14
300	Pasadena Beach	G12	1972	5
301	Black Bank	F11	1972	5
302	Stag Lake	F12	1979	1,278
	TOTAL (15)			2,315

N/A = Not available

Natural Scenic Attractions

Nineteen parks with special scenic qualities or natural significance are developed throughout the province. Development consists of parking lots, walking trails and in some cases, interpretative facilities. These sites are operated by staff from nearby camping parks. Picnicking is allowed, but camping is not.

TABLE 18 — NATURAL SCENIC ATTRACTIONS NEWFOUNDLAND AND LABRADOR

MAP REF.	NAME	GRID/LOCATION	YEAR OPENED	SIZE (ha)
303	Cataracts	E16	1959	12
304	Point La Haye	D16	1972	19
305	Gooseberry Cove	E15	1972	3
306	Salmon Cove Sands	E16	1972	8
307	Topsail Beach	E17	1975	37
308	Middle Cove	E17	1972	3
309	Jiggin Head	F16	1979	4
310	Rattle Falls	F16	1979	21
311	Dungeon	F16	1980	2
312	Maberly	F16	1980	1
313	French Islands	D14	1982	2
314	Deadman's Bay	G16	1972	72
315	Indian Cove Neck	G15	1972	29
316	Northeast Arm	F16	1979	3
317	Eastport North	F16	1983	8
318	The Arches	H12	1979	13
319	Bottle Cove	G11	1972	27
320	Point au Mal	F11	1972	32
321	Codroy Valley	E10	1972	24
	TOTAL (19)			320

Ecological Reserves

Ecological Reserves in the Atlantic Region had their beginnings with the inception of the International Biological Program (IBP). The IBP was a ten year (1964-1974) cooperative project between the International Council of Scientific Unions and fifty-eight participating nations. Its role was to study the biological productivity of the earth and relate this to human adaptability and welfare. The program was a response by scientists and governments to the world-wide problems of human population explosion, food shortages, and environmental destruction. The IBP had seven sections: six were devoted to research on biological productivity or on man himself; the seventh was devoted to the conservation of terrestrial communities (CT). Each nation had an IBP committee with subcommittees for each section of the program in which the nation was taking part. National IBP committees were funded through and responsible to nationally funded scientific organizations. In Canada, IBP was under the direction of a committee representing senior university and government research scientists appointed by the National Research Council.

The Organization of IBP-CT in Canada was as follows: Canada was divided into ten regions, each with a Scientific Advisory Panel. Each consulting panel had two co-chairmen who in turn made up the national CT subcommittee. Regions 1 to 6 each coincided with a province from British Columbia to Quebec. Region 7 encompassed the three Maritime Provinces; Region 8, Newfoundland and Labrador. Region 9 encompassed the Yukon; Region 10, the NWT.

The objective of the Canadian CT subcommittee was not only to locate examples of the major ecosystems in Canada, but also to work toward their protection as Ecological Reserves.

Sites surveyed for IBP-CT and recommended as Ecological Reserves had no special legal status. Since that time, the provinces of New Brunswick, Nova Scotia, and Newfoundland and Labrador have enacted special legislation to establish Ecological Reserves. Currently they are reviewing candidate sites for formal recognition and in New Brunswick and Newfoundland, some have been formally proclaimed. Prince Edward Island has conducted a study and review of areas, but has not yet decided on a mechanism for formal establishment.

Red Pine Stand, Blue Mountain Ecological Reserve

ECOLOGICAL RESERVES — NEW BRUNSWICK

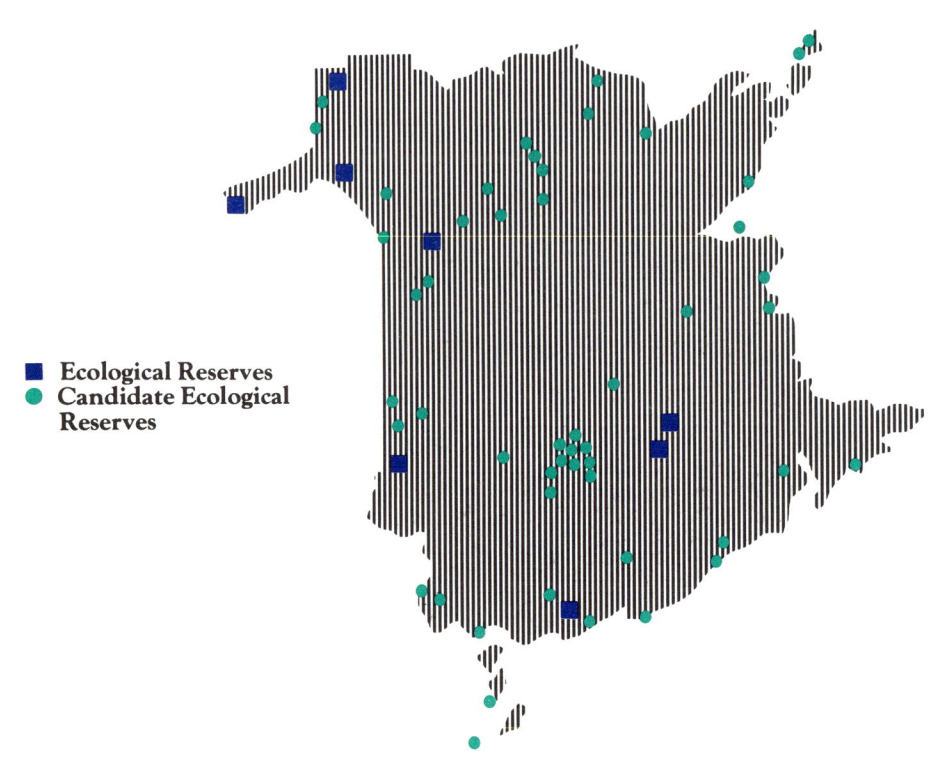

■ Ecological Reserves
● Candidate Ecological Reserves

The Province of New Brunswick passed its Ecological Reserves Act in 1975 and it came into effect on April 1, 1976. The Lieutenant-Governor in Council, on the recommendation of the Minister of Natural Resources, may establish ecological reserves either on private or Crown land. Reserves on private land are acquired by agreement, lease or exchange. An Advisory Council has been established to study and report on any matters pertaining to the act, and to conduct public hearings with respect to the establishment, abolishment or change in boundary lines of an ecological reserve.

Regulations require that a management plan be prepared describing in detail the natural and cultural resources for each ecological reserve. The plan must also describe the terms, conditions and restrictions upon which entry, activities or works are permissable within the bounds of an ecological reserve.

Generally, regulations are quite restrictive. Casual use in the form of hunting or trapping is permitted, but habitat modification through timber cutting or other resource development is strictly prohibited.

Twenty-seven potential ecological reserves were originally identified under the International Biological Program in 1971 and 1972. Subsequently, the Department of Natural Resources continued the investigation and identified an additional thirty-eight sites by 1975. Two sites have since been found unsuitable and have therefore been deleted.

As a result, a total of sixty-three sites represents the current inventory of candidate ecological reserves in the Province of New Brunswick. To date, seven of these areas have received formal designation under the Ecological Reserves Act and one is pending. Work is continuing both on the identification of new candidate sites and on the formal establishment of ecological reserves. The province is working towards the establishment of a system of ecological reserves which will represent New Brunswick's ecological diversity.

The following tables separately identify formally declared and candidate ecological reserves in New Brunswick. Note that candidate reserves have no protective status unless they fall within the bounds of an existing protected area such as a national park or federal migratory bird sanctuary.

TABLE 19   ECOLOGICAL RESERVES — NEW BRUNSWICK

MAP REF.	NAME	GRID/ LOCATION	YEAR EST.	SIZE (ha)	ECOSYSTEM
322	Lock Alva Lake	C3	1979	12	Mature red spruce community
323	Cranberry Lake	D4	1979	47	Extensive red oak community
324	Phillipstown	D4	1979	8	Great blue heron nesting site
325	Oak Mountain	C2	(P)	100	Sugar maple-beech association
326	Blue Mountain	E2	1976	50	Even-aged red pine stand
327	Glazier Lake	E1	1976	97	Mixed forest
328	McCoy Brook	E1	1976	43	Mixed hardwood stand
329	South Kedgwick River	E1	1976	54	Black spruce forest
	TOTAL (8)			411	

(P) — Provisional Reserve

Mixed Forest, Glazier Lake Ecological Reserve

TABLE 20　CANDIDATE ECOLOGICAL RESERVES — NEW BRUNSWICK

MAP REF.	NAME	GRID/ LOCATION	SIZE (ha)	ECOSYSTEM
330	St. Croix River Islands	C2	19	Forested and grassland islands, freshwater marsh
331	Little Salmon River Gorge	C4	225	Steep river gorge
332	Picadilly Mountain	C4	132	Mixed hardwood forest
333	Jolicure Lake	C5	120	Peatland bog
334	Gilbert Island	C3	240	River island floodplain
335	Narrows Mountain	D2	42	Tolerant sugar maple-beech association
336	Long Lake	D2	325	Lowland softwoods, hardwood ridges
337	Stewart Plain	D2	24	Even-aged red pine stand
338	Shea Lake	D2	36	Climax eastern hemlock stand
339	First Lake	E1	32	Balsam fir community
340	Campobello's Liberty Point	B3	36	Wind-dominated climax-vegetation
341	South-east Upsalquitch	E3	75	Mixed coniferous forest
342	Upsalquitch River	E3	34	Young jack pine, red pine association
343	McDougalls Brook	E3	57	Relic white pine stand
344	Hardwood Island	C2	15	Offshore island, diverse avian population
345	Miscou Island Shoreline	E5	45	Shoreline, sand dune system
346	Portage Island	E5	465	Offshore island community
347	Ayers Lake	D2	70	Clear lake, old conifer forest
348	McManus Hill	C5	13	Rich hardwood forest
349	Cape Spencer	C4	140	Coastal system, rocky cliffs
350	Little Toomowa Lake	C3	87	Bog, shallow lake
351	Bald Peak	E2	38	Mountain peak, treeless talus slopes
352	Sweat Hill	E3	300	Even-aged balsam fir stand
353	Lower McNair Brook	E3	50	Mixed coniferous forest
354	Tabusintac Blacklands	E5	124	Black spruce, jack pine, osprey, blue heron
355	Kouchibouguac Lagoon	D5	135	Salt marsh, sand dunes
356	Little Semiwagan Brook	D4	65	Cedar swamp, mixed forest, deer, moose

CANDIDATE ECOLOGICAL RESERVES — NEW BRUNSWICK (cont'd)

MAP REF.	NAME	GRID/ LOCATION	SIZE (ha)	ECOSYSTEM
357	Mountain Brook	D3	65	Mature mixed forest
358	Mount Elizabeth	E3	83	Open black spruce forest, talus slopes
359	Wilson Brook	C5	27	Rare plant habitat, gypsum cliffs
360	Musquash Salt Marsh	C3	654	Saltwater marsh
361	Machias Seal Island	B2	12	Coastal island, seabird nesting colonies
362	Baillie Settlement	C2	12	Eastern white cedar stand
363	Hampton Forest	C4	43	Forested talus stand
364	Hampton Marsh	C4	1,197	Freshwater marsh
365	Kouchibouguac Sand Dunes	D5	140	Barrier island, sand dunes
366	Sunpoke Lake	C3	913	Freshwater marsh and lake
367	Portobello Creek	C3	4,093	Freshwater marsh and floodplain forest
368	Acadia Forest (1)	C3	27	Black spruce forest
369	Acadia Forest (2)	C3	27	Black spruce forest
370	Acadia Forest (3)	D3	39	Balsam fir forest community
371	Acadia Forest (4)	D3	19	Black spruce forest
372	Bull Pasture Bog	D3	403	Sphagnum bog
373	Acadia Forest (5)	D3	23	Sugar maple-red maple forest
374	Acadia Forest (6)	D3	4	Red maple-white birch forest
375	Currie Mountain	D3	19	Mixed wood forest
376	Payson Lake	D2	51	Dystrophic lake, eastern white cedar
377	Moody Hill	D2	71	Deciduous forest community
378	Grand Falls Gorge	E2	15	White spruce, white birch, rare arctic-alpine plants
379	Veneer	E2	43	Old-growth deciduous forest
380	Green River	E1	2,017	Old-growth balsam fir forest
381	Heron Island	E3	22	Bird nesting colony, coastal island
382	Peters River	E4	71	Salt marsh
383	Miscou Island	E5	770	Coastal sphagnum bog
384	Nepisiquit Lakes	E3	23	Red pine stand
TOTAL (55)			13,827	

ECOLOGICAL RESERVES — NOVA SCOTIA

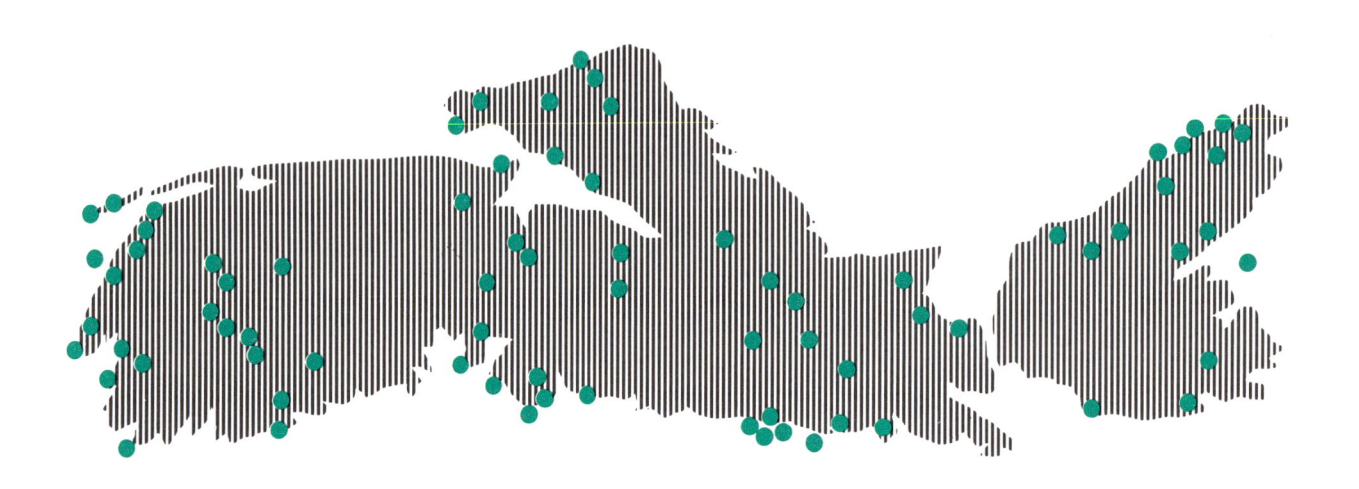

Nova Scotia is currently evaluating the sixty-nine sites originally identified under the International Biological Program in the early 1970's, as well as seven other sites that have been identified since that time. They are included in a recent study carried out by the Nova Scotia Museum and Department of Lands and Forests which has resulted in a comprehensive report, **Natural History of Nova Scotia.** This will form the basis for identifying and determining the relative importance of sites. Eighteen sites are protected within the boundaries of national parks, provincial parks and other conservation areas. Another twenty-four are largely on crown land and are given some protection. It is intended that a number of sites will be protected under the Special Places Act (1981), but to date none have been formally designated. An Advisory Committee has been appointed to oversee the process of selection and designation of sites. Some sites may also be recommended for protection as Natural Environment Parks under the Provincial Parks system. The following table includes the original sixty-nine IBP sites and the seven additional sites that are being considered for protection by the Province.

Coastal Habitats at Conrad Island

TABLE 21 CANDIDATE ECOLOGICAL RESERVES — NOVA SCOTIA

MAP REF.	NAME	GRID/ LOCATION	SIZE (ha)	ECOSYSTEM
385	Cape D'Or	C5	38.8	Arctic-alpine habitat
386	Shulie River	C5	31.2	Red spruce forest
387	Chignecto	C5	31.2	Red pine forest
388	John Lusby National Wildlife Area	C5	652.8	Salt marsh
389	Fenwick	C5	73.7	Deciduous forest
390	Black River Road	C5	23.1	Jack pine forest
391	Moose River	C5	323.7	Red spruce forest
392	Economy River	C6	77.7	Old-growth red spruce forest
393	Kemptown	C6	0.4	River intervale, rare plants
394	Glencoe	C7	0.8	River intervale, rare plants
395	Clydesdale	C8	77.7	Deciduous forest
396	Black River	D8	303.5	Alkaline bog
397	Piper Glen	D8	27.1	Mixed forest
398	Lake O'Law	D9	34.8	Old-growth deciduous and coniferous forests
399	Second Fork Brook	D9	58.3	Old-growth deciduous forest
400	Petit-Etang	D9	93.1	Eutrophic marsh
401	French Mountain Lake	D9	54.2	Lake and bogs
402	French Mountain Bog	D9	15.4	Sphagnum bog
403	Grande Anse River	D9	1,618.7	Old-growth deciduous forest
404	Sunday Lake	D9	6,021.7	Boreal forest, barrens and bogs
405	North Aspy River	D9	256.6	Old-growth deciduous forest
406	French River	D9	89.4	Old-growth mixed forest
407	Oregon	D9	19.4	Old-growth hemlock forest
408	Bird Islands	D9	62.3	Bird nesting site
409	Marion Bridge	C9	54.2	Deciduous forest
410	Point Michaud	C9	159.0	Beach and sand dunes
411	Melrose	C7	26.3	Old-growth hemlock forest
412	Bickerton Island	C8	12.1	Bird nesting site
413	Tobacco Island	B8	10.1	Bird nesting site
414	Little White Island	B7	7.7	Bird nesting site
415	Abraham Lake	C7	50.6	Red spruce forest
416	Brokenback Island	B7	5.7	Bird nesting site

CANDIDATE ECOLOGICAL RESERVES — NOVA SCOTIA (cont'd)

MAP REF.	NAME	GRID/ LOCATION	SIZE (ha)	ECOSYSTEM
417	Long Island	B7	4.0	Bird nesting site
418	Pumpkin Island	B7	6.5	Bird nesting site
419	Horse Island	B7	6.1	Coastal island
420	Conrad Beach	B6	34.8	Barrier sand dunes
421	Kidston Lake	B6	54.2	Barrens, rare plants
422	Bear Cove	B6	7.7	Sphagnum bog
423	Duncan's Cove	B6	221.4	Coastal barrens
424	West Dover	B6	182.1	Coastal barrens and bogs
425	Hollahan Lake	B5	4.0	Jack pine forest
426	Burnaby Lake	B5	38.8	Red spruce forest
427	Shelburne River	B4	62.3	Old-growth hemlock forest
428	Sixth Lake	B4	80.9	Hemlock-red spruce forest
429	Broad River	A5	50.6	Red spruce forest
430	Carter's Beach	A5	38.8	Sand dunes
431	Silvery Lake	B4	8.1	Old-growth hemlock forest
432	Shelburne Barrens	A4	5,652.7	Fire barrens
433	Sandhills Beach	A4	20.2	Sand dunes and salt marsh
434	Quinan Lake	A4	536.2	Old-growth mixed forest
435	Moses Lake	A4	11.7	Old-growth deciduous forest
436	Spinney's Heath	A4	279.6	Sphagnum bog
437	Chebogue Lake	A3	116.5	Tidal lake
438	Hectanooga	B3	62.3	Eastern white cedar swamp
439	Cape Saint Mary	B3	131.5	Sand dunes and salt marsh
440	Placid Lake	B4	174.8	Lake and old-growth hemlock forest
441	Belliveau Lake	B3	299.4	Lake and rare plants
442	Grosses Coques	B3	50.6	Salt marsh
443	Brier Island	B3	137.6	Sedge and sphagnum bogs
444	Central Bog	B3	97.1	Sphagnum bog
445	Birch Lake	B4	161.9	Old-growth white pine forest
446	Sporting Lake	B4	32.4	Old-growth hemlock-pine forest
447	Big Dam Lake	B4	151.8	Old-growth hemlock forest
448	Kentville Ravine	C5	38.8	Old-growth hemlock forest

Bloodroot (Sanguinaria Canadensis)

CANDIDATE ECOLOGICAL RESERVES — NOVA SCOTIA (cont'd)

MAP REF.	NAME	GRID/ LOCATION	SIZE (ha)	ECOSYSTEM
449	Cape Split	C5	445.2	Deciduous forest and arctic-alpine habitat
450	Saint Croix River	B5	121.4	Mixed forest and rare plants
451	Shady Brook	B5	89.0	Red spruce-hemlock forest
452	Shubenacadie	C6	14.2	Rare plants
453	South Maitland	C6	147.7	Gypsum cave and river intervale
454	Pomquet Beach	C8	233.0	Barrier sand dunes
455	Frankville	C8	50.0	Mixed forest
456	Indian Man Lake	C7	40.0	Oak-pine forest
457	Gabarus-Belfry Gut	C9	890.0	Barrier beach
458	Gillfillian Lake	A4	188.0	Coastal plain, rare plants
459	Wight Nature Preserve	B5	16.0	Bog, barrens, mixed forest
460	Meander River	C6	N/A	River intervale, rare plants
	TOTAL (76)		21,301.2	

N/A = Not available

ECOLOGICAL RESERVES — PRINCE EDWARD ISLAND

Fourteen sites were identified in Prince Edward Island under the International Biological Program in the early 1970's. Because the island is ninety-eight percent privately owned it has been difficult for the government to acquire many of these areas, with the result that some have deteriorated substantially due to human modification. Nevertheless, in 1982 the Prince Edward Island government commissioned a study by the University of Prince Edward Island which reommends thirty-six sites for protection as natural areas, including many of the original IBP sites. Some of these areas are protected within existing parks or sanctuaries, or are crown owned and therefore development may be controlled. The province is currently considering ways in which the remaining areas can be protected.

TABLE 22 — CANDIDATE NATURAL AREAS — PRINCE EDWARD ISLAND

MAP REF.	NAME	GRID/LOCATION	ECOSYSTEM
461	Hog Island System* (a) Kildare Sand Hills (b) Cascumpec Sand Hills (c) Conway Sand Hills (d) Malpeque Sand Hills	D6	Sand dunes, barrier islands
462	Cable Head	D7	Sand dunes
463	Point Deroche	D7	Sand dunes, barrier-beach pond
464	Basin Head*	D7	Old sand dune system
465	Black Pond*	D7	Sand dune system/barrier beach pond
466	South Lake*	D7	Sand dune system, barrier beach pond
467	Little Courtin Island	D6	Offshore Island, migratory birds

CANDIDATE NATURAL AREAS — PRINCE EDWARD ISLAND (cont'd)

MAP REF.	NAME	GRID/LOCATION	ECOSYSTEM
468	Murray Islands*	D7	Colonial nesting birds
469	Oultons Island	D5	Colonial nesting birds
470	Bunbury Island	D6	Colonial nesting birds
471	Grover (Ram) Island	D6	Colonial nesting birds
472	George Island	D6	Colonial nesting birds
473	St. Peters Island	D6	Colonial nesting birds
474	Boughton Island	D7	Colonial nesting birds
475	Haliburton	D5	Hardwood forest
476	Murray River Pines*	D7	Red pine
477	Townshend Woodlot	D7	Hardwood forest, yellow birch, beech, sugar-maple
478	Royalty Oaks	D6	Oak stand
479	Richmond	D6	White ash stand
480	Pinette*	D7	Hemlock forest
481	Canavoy Pines	D7	Red pine
482	Brudenell River Pines	D7	White pine
483	Canavoy Red Oaks	D7	Red oak
484	Locke Road Jack Pine	D5	Jack pine
485	St. Chrysostome Cedars	D5	Eastern cedar
486	Naufrage River	D7	Pristine River system
487	Miminegash River	D5	Pristine River system
488	Trout Creek	D5	Salt marsh
489	Salutation Cove	D6	Salt marsh
490	Degros Marsh	D7	Salt marsh, tidal pond
491	Tryon River	D6	Salt marsh
492	Pisquid Pond	D7	Freshwater pond
493	Afton Lake	D7	Freshwater pond
494	O'Keefe Lake	D7	Freshwater pond
495	Miscouche Bog*	D6	Sphagnum bog
496	East Baltic Bog	D7	Sphagnum bog
	TOTAL (36)		

*Original International Biological Program Sites (1974)

ECOLOGICAL RESERVES — NEWFOUNDLAND AND LABRADOR

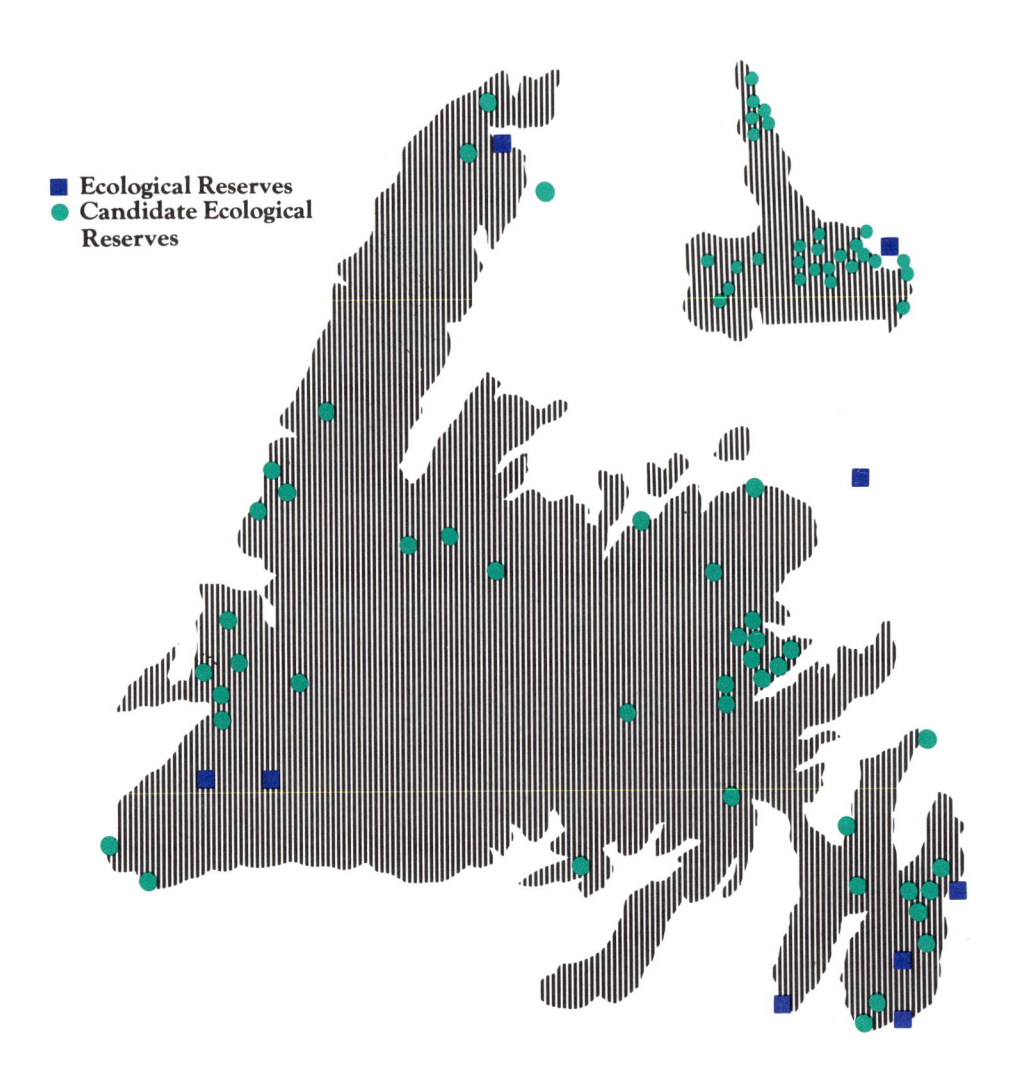

■ Ecological Reserves
● Candidate Ecological Reserves

In 1980, Newfoundland passed the Wilderness and Ecological Reserves Act to provide for natural areas in the province to be set aside "for the benefit, education and enjoyment of present and future generations in the province". Under this act a Wilderness and Ecological Reserves Advisory Council has been established to advise the Lieutenant-Governor in Council, through the Minister of Culture, Recreation and Youth, on all matters in relation to the establishment, management and termination of reserves. The Advisory Council consists of up to eleven members, with at least six of these representing the public.

General regulations prohibit fishing, hunting, trapping, use of vehicles and any form of modification to the natural environment.

As one basis for the selection of candidate ecological reserves, the province is using the eighty sites identified under the International Biological Program. As well, the general public is encouraged to submit suggestions on sites for consideration. All sites are reviewed and as documentation becomes complete, they may be forwarded to the Advisory Council for consideration as Ecological Reserves. Currently there are five areas which have been formally set aside. Three areas have also been set aside as provisional reserves which provide interim protection until a public hearing can be completed and a report made to Cabinet.

One other area, the Central Avalon Wilderness Area, was originally created pursuant to the Wild Life Act, and was managed using wildlife reserve regulations. It was recently converted to Provisional Wilderness Area status under the new legislation.

TABLE 23   ECOLOGICAL RESERVES — NEWFOUNDLAND AND LABRADOR

MAP REF.	NAME	GRID/ LOCATION	YEAR EST.	SIZE (Sq. Kms)	ECOSYSTEM
497	Cape St. Mary's	D15	1983	3.4	Seabird nesting habitat, gannets, murres, puffins
498	Witless Bay Islands	E17	1983	3.0	Seabird nesting habitat, murres, puffins, razor-bills
499	Funk Island	G16	1983	0.26	Seabird nesting habitat, murres, gannets, razor-bills
500	Hare Bay Islands	I14	1983	6.5	Eider ducks, seabirds
501	Gannet Islands	X3	1983	0.81	Coastal barrens, puffins
502	The Grass/Robinson's River	F11	(P)	11.0	Natural grassland, flood plain
503	King George IV Lake Delta	F12	(P)	18.6	Delta system, waterfowl nesting area
504	Mistaken Point	D16	(P)	2.5	Precambrian fossil site
505	Avalon Wilderness	E16	(PW)	1,217.3	Forest, peatlands, barrens
	TOTAL (9)			1,263.37	

(P)   = Provisional
(PW) = Provisional Wilderness Area

Cape St. Mary's Ecological Reserve

TABLE 24 — CANDIDATE ECOLOGICAL RESERVES NEWFOUNDLAND AND LABRADOR

MAP REF.	NAME	GRID/ LOCATION	SIZE (Sq. Kms)	ECOSYSTEM
506	Baccalieu Island	F17	N/A	Seabird nesting habitat
507	Northern Peninsula Barrens	I13	57	Coastal barrens, peatlands, forest
508	Long Range Mountains	G12	900	Alpine barrens, krummholz
509	Serpentine Lake	F11	77	Serpentine barrens, forest peatlands
510	Table Mountain Plateau	F11	9.6	Coastal barrens, krummholz
511	Grand Lake Brook	F11	1.5	Fens, swamp, maple, black spruce
512	Little Grand Lake	F12	64	Pine marten habitat
513	Coal All Island	G15	0.26	Salt marsh
514	Burnt Berry Brook	G13	1	Lichen forest, red pine
515	Little Gander Pond	F14	3	Natural forest (uncut)
516	Red Cove Barrens	E14	32	Coastal barrens, heathlands, peatland
517	Mint Brook	F15	1.5	Lichen forest
518	Gambo Pond (Pine Acres)	F15	3	Lichen forest, red pine
519	Terra Nova (Georges Pond)	F15	2	Red pine stand
520	Southern Avalon Barrens	D16	32	Coastal barrens
521	Crooked Bog	G13	6	Peatland, oceanic raised bog
522	Ladle Cove Bog	G15	9	Bog plateau, black spruce forest
523	Browmoore Bog	F11	29	Blanket bog and bog plateau
524	Cape Ray Barrens	E10	10	Coastal barrens
525	Port Aux Basques Barrens	E10	80	Coastal barrens, blanket bogs
526	Baker's Brook Bog	G12	11	Bog plateau, black spruce forest
527	Trout River Plateau Bog	G12	25	String fen
528	La Manche Bog	E17	1.5	Blanket bog
529	Groais Island Bird Rock	H14	N/A	Razor-billed auks
530	Big Brook Estuary	F16	5.2	Coastal vegetation, peatland, balsam fir forest

CANDIDATE ECOLOGICAL RESERVES — NEWFOUNDLAND AND LABRADOR (cont'd)

MAP REF.	NAME	GRID/ LOCATION	SIZE (Sq. Kms)	ECOSYSTEM
531	Sandy Lake	G13	0.75	Red pine, lichen forest
532	Big Brook Barrens	I13	0.25	Coastal barrens
533	Jonathan's Pond	G15	1.5	White birch
534	Memorial University Forest Reserve Area	E17	17	Balsam fir
535	Menihek Lake	X1	35	Lichen forest, white spruce
536	Red Bay Barrens	X3	18	Coastal barrens, krummholz, peatland
537	Seven Plumes Falls	X2	0.05	Spray zone
538	Island Pond	E16	0.6	Black spruce forest, fen
539	Upper Fraser River Canyon	Y2	2	Coniferous forest, black spruce
540	Witless Bay Line Fen	E17	14	Mire complex, string fen, slope fen, slope bog

Pine Marten

CANDIDATE ECOLOGICAL RESERVES — NEWFOUNDLAND AND LABRADOR (cont'd)

MAP REF.	NAME	GRID/ LOCATION	SIZE (Sq. Kms)	ECOSYSTEM
541	Peter's River Fen	D16	0.02	Slope fen
542	Terra Nova Fen	F15	0.005	Slope fen
543	Long Pond Fen	E15	0.7	Slope fen
544	New Harbour Barrens	E16	10.4	Barrens
545	Hawke Hills	E16	13	Barrens, arctic-alpine species, krummholz, heathlands
546	Lower Churchill River	X2	30	Lichen forest, black spruce
547	Susan and Beaver Rivers	X2	71	Black spruce, balsam fir, birch
548	Gull Island Lake	X2	73	Black spruce forest
549	Smaller Partridge River	X3	65	White spruce, poplar forest
550	Lac Joseph Forest	X2	N/A	Birch forest
551	Eagle River Headwaters	X3	520	String fens, osprey and bald eagle
552	Seven Islands Bay Valleys	Y2	N/A	Birch forest valleys
553	Red Wine River Mountains	X2	234	Lichen forest, caribou wintering
554	Mealy Mountains	X3	1,040	Barrens, caribou wintering and breeding
555	Churchill Falls	X2	0.7	Forest, fen, spray influence
556	Lac Joseph	X1	N/A	Spring bogs
557	Okak Bay Palsa Bog	Y2	N/A	Palsa bog
558	Jack Pine Lake Palsa Bog	Y2	N/A	Palsa bog
559	East Pompey Island	X3	2	Coastal vegetation, barrens, arctic hares
560	Devil's Lookout Island	X3	0.81	Peregrine falcon, coastal barrens, krummholz
561	Bird Islands	X3	0.18	Puffins, razor-billed auks, murres
562	Cape Porcupine Strand	X3	20	Strand vegetation, black spruce forest
563	Naskaupi River	X2	40	Black spruce, baslam fir

CANDIDATE ECOLOGICAL RESERVES — NEWFOUNDLAND AND LABRADOR (cont'd)

MAP REF.	NAME	GRID/ LOCATION	SIZE (Sq. Kms)	ECOSYSTEM
564	No Name Lake	X3	65	Black spruce, string fens, osprey, bald eagle
565	Tinker Harbour	X3	4	Intertidal mud, strand vegetation
566	Snegamook Lake	X2	195	Black spruce, fen, osprey, Canada geese
567	Thomas Falls	X2	N/A	Canyon-bryophyte vegetation
568	Middle Brook	F15	0.5	Lichen forest
569	Barachois Pond	F11	7.8	Balsam fir, yellow birch, black ash
570	Big Brook Forest	F16	1.4	Lichen forest
571	White Islets	F16	0.2	Coastal barrens, balsam fir
572	Terra Nova National Park	F15	394	Second growth forest, peatland
573	Refuge Bay (Mount Thoresbey)	Y2	40	Vegetation change with elevation
574	Village Bay Peninsula	Y2	7	Coastal barrens, fossil sand dunes
575	Shell Island	X3	0.5	Coastal barrens, peatlands
576	Mobile Big Pond	E17	18	Second-growth forest, peatland
577	Gros Morne National Park	G12	1,942	Forest, peatland, barrens
	TOTAL (72)		6,245.93	

N/A = Not available

White-tailed deer

Provincial Wildlife Management Areas
Wildlife Refuges/Game Sanctuaries

New Brunswick, Nova Scotia and Prince Edward Island each contain a number of areas set aside to protect certain wildlife species and their habitat. Many of the older areas were created to provide reservoirs for wildlife in hope that game species would multiply and expand into surrounding areas. More recently a number of areas have been established to permit more active and flexible management. Each province has a slightly different philosophy and approach to establishing and managing wildlife areas. Some concentrate on waterfowl production and habitat, while others have a combination of areas for both mammals and waterfowl.

Newfoundland and Labrador previously had a series of game sanctuaries, principally to protect nesting colonies of seabirds. These areas were converted to ecological reserves when new, more appropriate legislation was promulgated in 1980. Nevertheless, game sanctuary legislation still exists, and some thought is being given to the establishment of new sanctuaries.

Acadian Village Wildlife Management Area

Wildlife Management Areas/Wildlife Refuges — New Brunswick

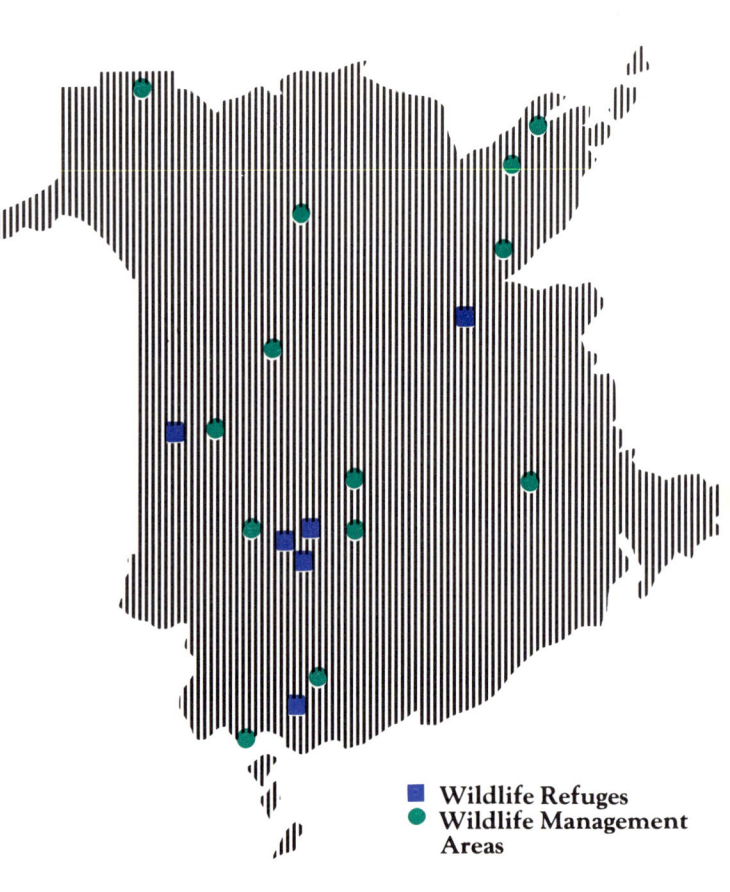

Currently there are six wildlife refuges and thirteen wildlife management areas in New Brunswick. Both types of areas were recently gazetted in Regulation 82-4, passed by the Lieutenant-Governor in Council under Section 118 of the Fish and Wildlife Act. Game refuges have been in existence in the province since 1919 when the New Brunswick Game Refuge was established. Unfortunately, records have not revealed where this refuge was located or why it apparently was deleted, but Canaan River Game Refuge, established in 1921, is still in existence today (although it is now a wildlife management area). Over the years there has been a gradual conversion of game refuges to game management areas, and the word "game" has been supplanted by the more applicable word "wildlife". The refuges which remain are generally small areas which are intended to be used in the interest of public education. Fredericton wildlife refuge, for example, is within city limits and provides opportunities for public viewing of waterfowl and other wildlife. Wildlife Management Areas are converted game refuges and are vestiges of an outdated theory of producing surplus game for surrounding areas. However, as wildlife management areas they permit greater flexibility in terms of management techniques and have recently been used for wildlife studies. It is unlikely that any new, large wildlife

■ Wildlife Refuges
● Wildlife Management Areas

management areas will be established, though smaller areas may continue to be set aside for educational purposes.

TABLE 25	WILDLIFE REFUGES — NEW BRUNSWICK			
MAP REF.	NAME	GRID/ LOCATION	YEAR EST.	SIZE (Sq. Kms)
578	O'Dell	C3	1949	1.4
579	Univ. of New Brunswick	C3	1949	15.2
580	Utopia	C3	1940	31.0
581	Kindness Club	D2	1964	0.07
582	Fredericton	C3	1963	1.3
583	Wilson's Point	D4	1950	0.5
	TOTAL (6)			49.47

TABLE 26	WILDLIFE MANAGEMENT AREAS — NEW BRUNSWICK			
MAP REF.	NAME	GRID/ LOCATION	YEAR EST.	SIZE (Sq. Kms)
584	Bantalor	D3	1930	152.9
585	Becaguimac	D2	1929	111.5
586	Burpee	D3	1934	181.7
587	Canaan River	D4	1921	225.5
588	Kedgwick	E2	1923	829.4
589	Lepreau River	C3	1927	243.7
590	Plaster Rock — Renous	D3	1939	842.4
591	Big Tracadie River	E4	1937	39.1
592	Mt. Carleton	E3	1975	198.3
593	Minister's Island	C2	1980	2.0
594	King's Landing	C2	1980	1.3
595	Acadian Village	E4	1980	9.7
596	MacDonald Farm	E4	1980	0.6
	TOTAL (13)			2,838.1

■ Game Sanctuaries
● Wildlife Management Areas

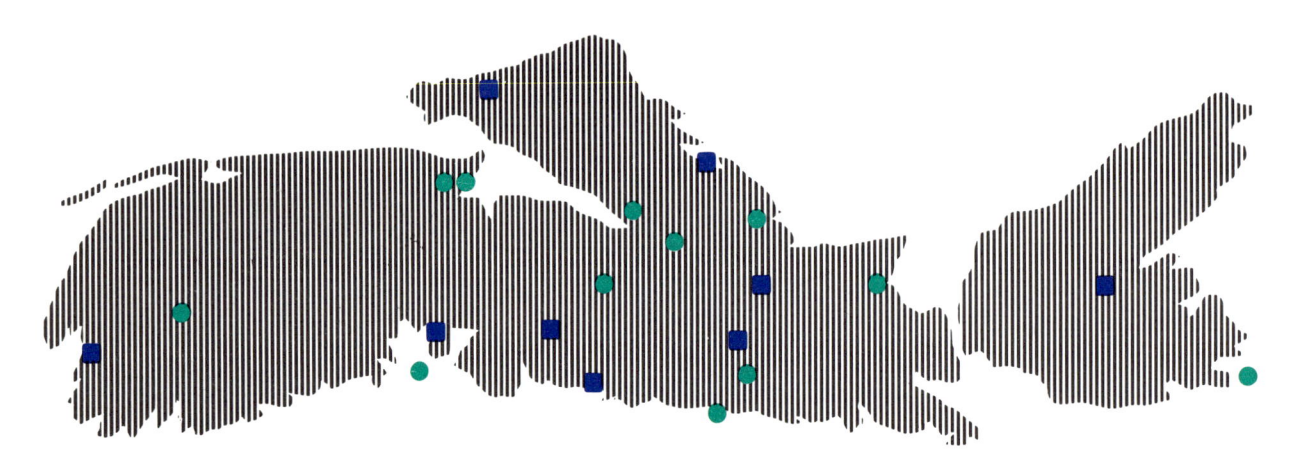

Game Sanctuaries and Wildlife Management Areas — Nova Scotia

Nova Scotia has ten game sanctuaries and twelve wildlife management areas, both designated by Order in Council pursuant to the Lands and Forests Act. The Lieutenant-Governor in Council, on recommendation from the Minister of Lands and Forests, can declare either private or public lands as game sanctuaries or wildlife management areas.

The first Nova Scotia **Game Sanctuary** was Waverley, established by Order in Council dated January 18, 1926, at the request of the Boy Scouts Association. The purpose of this sanctuary was to assist in the maintenance and preservation of the forests and in the protection of game. Later, game sanctuaries were established to allow game species to increase and to provide a reservoir which would allow game to spill out into surrounding forests. The latter approach met with little success and in 1968 it was recommended that the Tobeatic Game Sanctuary, originally established in 1927, be converted to a wildlife management area. This provides more flexible management and has fostered studies of beaver, bobcat, waterfowl, lake fertilization and fish production.

The general regulation for game sanctuaries states that it is unlawful to hunt, take or kill or attempt to take or kill any wildlife.

Waverley Game Sanctuary

Wildlife Management Areas are units of private or public land where flexible regulations apply to the management and harvesting of wildlife. They have been established in more recent years to protect wildlife and waterfowl habitat and to provide opportunities for natural history education and outdoor recreation.

TABLE 27		GAME SANCTUARIES — NOVA SCOTIA			
MAP REF.	NAME	GRID/ LOCATION	YEAR EST.	SIZE (ha)	PURPOSE
597	Chignecto	C5	1937	22,098.8	Wildlife protection
598	Liscomb	C7	1928	45,326.8	Wildlife protection
599	Sunnybrae	C7	1930	518.0	Outdoor recreation, boy scouts
600	Waverley	B6	1926	5,698.2	Outdoor recreation, boy scouts
601	Brule Point (W)	C6	1963	80.9	Goose resting area
602	Blandford (W)	B5	1959	223.0	Waterfowl resting area
603	Martinique Beach (W)	B6	1974	308.0	Migratory bird concentration and waterfowl wintering
604	Melbourne Lake (W)	A3	1963	223.9	Waterfowl concentration and wintering
605	Spectacle Island (W)	D9	1969	1.0	Colonial bird nesting
606	Upper Clements(+)	B4	1977	303.5	Wildlife park
	TOTAL (10)			74,782.1	

(W) = Waterfowl game sanctuary
(+) = Proclaimed as a game sanctuary but operated as a provincial wildlife park

TABLE 28		WILDLIFE MANAGEMENT AREAS — NOVA SCOTIA			
MAP REF.	NAME	GRID/ LOCATION	YEAR EST.	SIZE (ha)	PURPOSE
607	Abercrombie	C7	1977	141.7	Education, nature interpretation and study
608	Antigonish Harbour	C8	1968	140.0	Migratory bird feeding, nesting, staging, resting and waterfowl wintering
609	Debert	C6	1973	269.1	Waterfowl feeding, nesting, resting and viewing area
610	Dewey Creek*	C5	1982	55.4	Waterfowl nesting, feeding, staging and resting
611	Eastern Shore Islands	B7	1976	Unknown	Colonial bird nesting

612	Kelly Lake	C7	1977	437.5	Watershed protection and recreation
613	Manganese Mines	C6	1973	232.7	Nature interpretation and study
614	Minas Basin	C5	1977	186.2	Waterfowl resting area
615	Pearl Island	B5	1976	317.0	Colonial bird nesting
616	Scatarie Island	D10	1976	1,554.6	Wildlife experimentation (Arctic Species)
617	Shubenacadie*+	C6	1979	413.0	Wildlife and wildlife habitat research
618	Tobeatic	B4	1968	49,212.7	Wildlife and wildlife habitat research
	TOTAL (12)			52,959.9	

* = Also managed under agreement with Ducks Unlimited (Canada)
+ = Proclaimed as a wildlife management area, but a portion is operated as a provincial wildlife park

Wildlife Management Areas — Prince Edward Island

Wildlife Management Areas in Prince Edward Island are established to provide protected feeding and resting areas for waterfowl, particularly Canada geese, during migration. They also serve to improve hunting opportunities in the vicinity surrounding the wildlife management areas. As well they provide opportunities for bird watchers, photographers and naturalists to observe, photograph and study waterfowl.

They are designated by the Lieutenant-Governor in Council under the Fish and Game Protection Act (1959, revised 1966), and administered by the Fish and Wildlife Division, Department of Community and Cultural Affairs. They are most often created on private land under agreement with the owners.

There are currently four wildlife management areas in Prince Edward Island. Generally, hunting, trapping or other disturbance of wildlife is not permitted. In future, it is possible that more areas of wetland or upland habitat could be set aside to afford protection to the habitat they contain, to provide a means for managing areas for sustained waterfowl production, and to enhance harvest management.

Indian River Wildlife Management Area

TABLE 29   WILDLIFE MANAGMENT AREAS — PRINCE EDWARD ISLAND

MAP REF.	NAME	GRID/ LOCATION	YEAR EST.	SIZE (ha)	PURPOSE
619	Indian River	D6	1971	316	Waterfowl habitat
620	Moore's	D7	1975	480	Waterfowl habitat
621	Rollo Bay	D7	1978	760	Waterfowl habitat
622	Orwell Cove	D7	1974	852	Waterfowl habitat
	TOTAL (4)			2,408	

SUMMARY AND CONCLUSIONS

The following tables present summary information regarding the numbers and size of natural heritage areas in each province and for the entire Region.

It is evident from the large number of areas that are protected, or being considered for protection, that the governments and people of Atlantic Canada have a great deal to be proud of. As of the date of this publication, there are 376 formally designated natural heritage areas in Atlantic Canada, covering 10,274 square kilometres.

This is not the time, however, to rest on our past accomplishments and feel that the task is complete. As illustrated in Table 31, all formally designated areas taken together represent less than two percent of the region, and many of the 246 candidate areas may never be included. Even those areas which are designated do not receive equal degrees of protection. In some cases, improper resource management and inadequate enforcement can lead to the destruction of the natural values for which an area was originally set aside.

TABLE 30	NATURAL HERITAGE AREAS OCCURRENCE BY PROVINCE				
	NEW BRUNSWICK	NOVA SCOTIA	PRINCE EDWARD ISLAND	NEWFOUNDLAND/ LABRADOR	ATLANTIC REGION
National Parks	2	2	1	2	7
Natural Areas of Canadian Significance	(2)	(2)		(3)	(7)
Canadian Heritage Rivers	1				1
National Wildlife Areas	5	7			12
Federal Migratory Bird Santuaries	2	8	1	1	12
Provincial Parks	61	108	36	77	282
Ecological Reserves	8			9	17
Candidate Ecological Reserves	(55)	(76)	(36)	(72)	(239)
Wildlife Management Areas	13	12	4		29
Wildlife Refuges/ Game Sanctuaries	6	10			16
TOTAL	98 (57)	147 (78)	42 (36)	89 (75)	376 (246)

Areas in brackets ( ) are not formally designated

It is not always easy to resolve the often conflicting objectives of economic development and environmental protection, and when conflict occurs, the environment is invariably compromised. It is therefore imperative to reinforce our resolve to protect our natural heritage, as our future ultimately depends upon our ability to foster harmony between society and our environment. It is hoped that this publication will serve to make Atlantic Canadians more aware of their natural heritage, and that concerned individuals and agencies will continue to strive for the conservation and protection of the environment which we all share.

TABLE 31 — NATURAL HERITAGE AREAS TOTAL SIZE BY PROVINCE (SQ. KMS)

	NEW BRUNSWICK	NOVA SCOTIA	PRINCE EDWARD ISLAND	NEWFOUNDLAND/ LABRADOR	ATLANTIC REGION
National Parks	444	1,332	32	2,339	4,147
Natural Areas of Canadian Significance					
Canadian Heritage Rivers					
National Wildlife Areas	58	24			82
Federal Migratory Bird Santuaries	3	42	1	9	55
Provincial Parks	221	66	21	227	535
Ecological Reserves	4			1,263	1,267
Candidate Ecological Reserves					
Wildlife Management Areas	2,838	530	24		3,392
Wildlife Refuges/ Game Sanctuaries	49	747			796
TOTAL	3,617	2,741	78	3,838	10,274
Surface Area	73,437	55,491	5,657	404,518	539,103
Percent	4.93%	4.94%	1.38%	0.95%	1.91%

SELECTED REFERENCES FOR ADDITIONAL READING

NATIONAL PARKS

1. **Lothian, W.F.,** *A History of Canada's National Parks,* Parks Canada, Ottawa, 1982
2. **Parks Canada,** *National Parks Policy,* National Parks Branch, Parks Canada, Ottawa, 1964
3. **Parks Canada,** *National Marine Parks — Draft Policy,* National Parks Branch, Parks Canada, Ottawa, 1983
4. **Parks Canada,** *A National Marine Park Concept: West Isles New Brunswick Pilot Study,* Parks Canada/Tourism New Brunswick, Ottawa, 1982

NATURAL AREAS OF CANADIAN SIGNIFICANCE

1. **Parks Canada,** *National Parks System Planning Manual,* National and Historic Parks Branch, Parks Canada 1972, 149P.
2. **Parks Canada,** *Natural Areas of Canadian Significance — A Preliminary Study,* Parks System Planning Division, National Parks Branch Ottawa, 1977, 123P.

CANADIAN HERITAGE RIVERS

1. **Parks Canada,** *A Canadian Heritage Rivers System — Notes of Technical Discussions,* Planning Division, ARC Branch, Parks Canada, 1979. 51P.
2. **Parks Canada,** *A Canadian Heritage Rivers System — A Proposal Prepared by the Canadian Heritage Rivers Task Force — Final Report;* Planning Division, ARC Branch, Parks Canada, 1981. 46P.
3. **Tourism — New Brunswick,** *St. Croix River Nomination Document — Canadian Heritage River System;* Tourism New Brunswick, Community Improvement Corporation DPA Consultants Ltd., Fredericton, 1984. 32P.

NATIONAL WILDLIFE AREAS

1. **Barkhouse, H.P., Smith, A.D.** *A Preliminary Summary of Background Information on National Wildlife Areas in the Atlantic Region,* Canadian Wildlife Service Atlantic Region, Environment Canada, 1981. 46P.
2. **Canadian Wildlife Service,** *Guidelines for Wildlife Policy in Canada,* Environment Canada, Canadian Wildlife Service, Ottawa, 1982.

FEDERAL MIGRATORY BIRD SANCTUARIES

1. **Smith, A. D.,** *Review of Migratory Bird Sanctuaries in the Atlantic Region,* Canadian Wildlife Service Environment Canada, Atlantic Region, Internal Report, Sackville, N.B. 1985.

PROVINCIAL PARKS

1. **Boggs, G.D. Assoc. Ltd.** *Nova Scotia Parks and Recreation System Plan,* Report for Nova Scotia Department of Lands and Forests, Parks and Recreation Division, Oakville, 1976 228P.
2. **New Brunswick;** *New Brunswick Parks Statistical Reports* Tourism New Brunswick, Field Services Division, Fredericton, 1983. 46P.
3. **Newfoundland and Labrador** *Newfoundland and Labrador Provincial Parks Statistics, 1983;* Parks Division Department of Culture, Recreation and Youth, St. John's, 1983, 14P.
4. **Newfoundland and Labrador** *Provincial Parks and Reserves — Newfoundland* Parks Division, Department of Culture, Recreation and Youth, St. John's, 1981.
5. **Nova Scotia,** *A Summary of Provincial Campground Users' Characteristics,* Parks and Recreation Division, Department of Lands and Forests, Halifax, 1984. 47P.
6. **Prince Edward Island,** *Classification of Provincial Parks in Prince Edward Island,* Parks and Conservation Branch, Department of Tourism Parks and Conservation, 1974. 9P.

ECOLOGICAL RESERVES

1. **International Biological Program** — Conservation of Terrestrial Communities Report of Region 8: Newfoundland and Labrador, St. John's, 1974.
2. **Ogilvie, Robert;** *Important Ecological Sites in Nova Scotia* Nova Scotia Museum Curatorial Report Number 49, Nova Scotia Department of Education, Halifax, 1984. 34P.
3. **Prince Edward Island** *Prince Edward Island Natural Areas Survey;* an internal report prepared by the Biology Department, UPEI, for the Department of Forestry, Charlottetown, 1982. 100P.
4. **Simmons, M.; Davis, D.; Griffiths, L.; and Mueke, A.;** *Natural History of Nova Scotia,* Nova Scotia Departments of Education and Lands and Forests, Halifax, Two Volumes, 1984. 807P.

5. **Taschereau, P.M., ed.** *Ecological Reserves in the Maritimes*, Canadian Committee for the International Biological Program, Conservation of Terrestrial Communities Subcommittee, Region 7, Halifax 1974. 220P.
6. **Taschereau, P.M.** *The Status of Ecological Reserves in Canada*, IRES Research Paper 82-01, Institute for Resources and Environmental Studies, Dalhousie University, Halifax, 1982 116P.
7. **Wein, R. N.ed.** *Ecological Reserves in New Brunswick*, University of New Brunswick, Fredericton. 230P.
8. **Wein, R. N.ed.** *Ecological Reserves in New Brunswick, 1975 Field Work;* University of New Brunswick Fredericton. 65P.

GENERAL

1. **Maritime Resource Management Service,** Important Freshwater Wetlands and Coastal Wildlife Habitats of Nova Scotia, Department of Lands and Forests, Kentville, 1982.
2. **Maritime Resource Management Service,** Nova Scotia Land Information Index, compiled for the Land Use Data Issue Group, Nova Scotia Deputy Ministers' Committee on Land Use, Halifax, 1982.
3. **Maritime Resource Management Service,** New Brunswick Index on Land Data and Maps, Surveys and Mapping Committee, Department of Natural Resources, Fredericton, 1984.
4. **Newfoundland,** Resources Inventory for Newfoundland and Labrador, Department of Forest Resources and Lands, Land Management Division, St. John's, 1984. 300P.

PHOTOGRAPHS

Front Cover
James Steeves

11. Saltmarsh and lagoon, Kouchibouguac National Park
Roger Beardmore
12. Point Wolfe River at high tide, Fundy National Park
James Steeves
14. Mouth of Grafton Brook, Kejimkujik National Park
James Steeves
17. Ingonish Beach and Cape Smokey, Cape Breton Highlands National Park
Ted Grant
19. Cavendish Beach, Prince Edward Island National Park
Roger Beardmore
21. Western Brook Pond, Gros Morne National Park
Peter Hope
23. Blue Hills, Terra Nova National Park
James Steeves
24. Deer Island Archipelago, New Brunswick
Parks Canada
26. Southwest Head, Grand Manan Island, New Brunswick
Parks Canada
27. Mealy Mountains, Labrador
Parks Canada
28. Torngat Mountains, Labrador
Parks Canada
31. Canadian Heritage Rivers, Atlantic Region
Harry Hirvonen
33. Beaver Lodge, Portobello Creek National Wildlife Area, New Brunswick
Canadian Wildlife Service
33. Marsh Hawk
Canadian Wildlife Service
34. Tintamarre National Wildlife Area, New Brunswick
Canadian Wildlife Service
34. Canadian Lynx
Canadian Wildlife Service
35. Chignecto National Wildlife Area, Nova Scotia
Canadian Wildlife Service
35. Margaree Island National Wildlife, Nova Scotia
Canadian Wildlife Service
36. Sand Pond National Wildlife Area, Nova Scotia
Canadian Wildlife Service
39. Puffin, Machias Seal Island Migratory Bird Sanctuary, New Brunswick
Canadian Wildlife Service
40. Port Hebert Migratory Bird Sanctuary, Nova Scotia
Canadian Wildlife Service
42. Sable Island Ponies, Sable Island Migratory Bird Sanctuary, Nova Scotia
Canadian Wildlife Service
43. Black Pond Migratory Bird Sanctuary, Prince Edward Island
Canadian Wildlife Service
44. Canada Geese
Canadian Wildlife Service
48. Windsurfers, Mactaquac Provincial Park, New Brunswick
Tourism New Brunswick
49. Parlee Beach Provincial Park, New Brunswick
Tourism New Brunswick
51. Moose
Canadian Wildlife Service
53. Blomidon Provincial Park, Nova Scotia
Roger Beardmore
55. Crystal Crescent Beach Provincial Park, Nova Scotia
Roger Beardmore
57. Martinique Beach Provincial Park, Nova Scotia
Roger Beardmore
61. Red Point Provincial Park, Prince Edward Island
Wayne Barrett, PEI Tourism
64. Northern Bay Sands Provincial Park, Newfoundland
Parks Division, Newfoundland Department of Culture, Recreation and Youth
67. Red Pine Stand, Blue Mountain Ecological Reserve
New Brunswick Department of Natural Resources
69. Mixed Forest, Glazier Lake Ecological Reserve
New Brunswick Department of Natural Resources
72. Coastal Habitats at Conrad Island, Halifax County, Nova Scotia
Derek Davis, Nova Scotia Museum
75. Bloodroot (sanguinaria canadensis)
Nova Scotia Museum
79. Cape St. Mary's Ecological Reserve, Newfoundland
Canadian Wildlife Service
81. Pine Marten
Canadian Wildlife Service
83. White-tailed deer
Canadian Wildlife Service
84. Acadian Village Wildlife Management Area, New Brunswick
Fish and Wildlife Branch, New Brunswick Department of Natural Resources
86. Waverley Game Sanctuary
Nova Scotia Department of Lands and Forests
88. Indian River Wildlife Management Area, Prince Edward Island
Fish and Wildlife Division, Prince Edward Island